YORK HANDBOOKS

GENERAL EDITOR:
Professor A.N. Jeffares
(*University of Stirling*)

UNIVERSITY OF NOTTINGHAM

10 0394048 5

WITHDRAWN

FROM THE LIBRARY

READING THE SCREEN
An Introduction to Film Studies

John Izod

BA PH D (LEEDS)
Head of Department of Film and Media Studies,
University of Stirling

LONGMAN
YORK PRESS

Original photography for the plates by
Ronald Boyd Stewart A.B.I.P.P., A.I.M.B.I.

YORK PRESS
Immeuble Esseily, Place Riad Solh, Beirut.

LONGMAN GROUP UK LIMITED
Longman House, Burnt Mill, Harlow,
Essex CM20 2JE, England
and Associated Companies throughout the world.

© Librairie du Liban 1984

*All rights reserved; no part of this publication may be
reproduced, stored in a retrieval system, or transmitted
in any form or by any means, electronic, mechanical,
photocopying, recording, or otherwise, without
the prior written permission of the copyright owner.*

First published 1984
Reprinted 1989

ISBN 0-582-02252 5

Produced by Longman Group (FE) Ltd.
Printed in Hong Kong

Contents

Part 1

Introduction

THE EXPERIENCE OF WATCHING THE SCREEN seems to be enjoyed so naturally and readily that we do not think of it as something that has had in some way to be learnt. No viewer, before watching a film or a television programme, has to go through the long and weary process each of us has had to suffer in learning to read a book. Indeed where, at a certain stage in our getting used to it, reading seems nothing so much as hard work, watching a movie offers nothing but relaxation. This being so, what can be the use of a handbook which claims to teach us something we already know, and something we have been practising since childhood? Who needs help in reading the screen?

We may start by remarking that the skills called on in understanding films do not come with us at birth. A baby placed in front of a television set may find the patterns of light playing on the screen or the sounds coming from the speaker interesting for a while, but they appear to convey no particular meaning to him.* At about a year he pays attention to the images and sounds of things familiar to him, and if he knows a name, perhaps for a dog, calls all animals 'bow wow'. An older child watching the screen spends a lot of time asking his parents what this or that means, what is happening now, whether this man is going to kill the other, or whatever. The answers he gets not only satisfy his immediate question, but they also let him work out for himself how meaning is constructed in film. So although we do not study formally how to read the cinematic image, a good deal of informal learning goes into developing these skills. By the time an individual reaches adolescence, they have been practised so frequently that reading a film seems 'natural'. In actuality it is 'natural' only in the sense that anything we practise a great deal, become good at, and enjoy (driving a car for instance) becomes natural. In other words the skill has become a habit.

If an introduction to reading the screen can show us some of the things we have unwittingly come to understand about movies, this still leaves open the question why we should bother to make this habitual skill into conscious knowledge. After all, if everybody reads the screen almost without knowing it, why take the matter any further? Why not leave well alone? The short answer is that meaning in film is constructed, and it can

---

*For simplicity the masculine pronoun is used throughout, so it is worth remarking that film and television employ women as well as men at all levels of the industry, and in every kind of job.

be constructed in many different ways, all of which subtly alter the meaning that is conveyed. To learn something of the methods by which a film has been put together is to discover some of the means by which those who made it tried to shape the audience's understanding of it. It is to discover that our responses to what goes on have been organised not only by the events we watch, but to some extent also by the way those events are presented on the screen. Another way of putting this is to say that we discover that cinema is not a window opening directly onto the world.

Window on the world

Many of us have grown up with the notion that 'the camera never lies'. We know, of course, that it is possible to get up to all kinds of tricks with a camera, but the old catch phrase lives on because there remains in the minds of many people an unspoken assumption that what the camera shows will in normal circumstances be what the world offers to our eyes.

Taken to its logical conclusion this way of thinking about film and television results in the idea that the camera shows us things the way they are. And the word 'things' comes to include not only tables, chairs and doormats, but also the organisation of the social and cultural world. Thus the idea that the camera provides a window on the world might discreetly swell to the point where cinema and television, when they deal with the world of our societies, seem to claim to tell the whole truth about that world. Plainly this is not a claim which an audience will take seriously when it watches a film that could not be anything but fiction – a horror movie or a science fiction film, for instance. But when the camera turns on the world we live in, for instance in a television documentary, the claim is much more serious.

What we first need to recognise is that by definition no film can tell the whole truth about even a very limited subject. To take one aspect of the craft only, the film making crew, however honest, have no option but to shape the viewer's perception of their subject by giving preference to one point of view of it over another. The topic of point of view will receive detailed consideration in Part 3. For the moment it will suffice to mention two ways in which the selection of a point of view affects what is shown. They are closely connected. Firstly there is the placing of the camera, the obtaining of a literal point of view. And secondly there is the selection of an attitude to the subject portrayed.

A dramatic example of the way camera placing can alter the audience's own point of view is found in television coverage of street rioting. Images of the same riot can look very different – and one's view of the participants tends to shift – according to the placing of the camera. If the crew have managed to get behind the police lines, the rioters appear to be hurling stones and petrol bombs not only at them but at us. It makes them look particularly ugly and dangerous. Conversely, when the camera crew have set up behind the rioters, the police make their charge on us as well as on them. It can be seen that in such circumstances it would be very difficult to obtain an impartial point of view for the camera without placing the crew between the lines of combatants – hardly a safe place to be.

The police have well practised routines for covering civil riots, and they also have an organisation geared to the provision of such information as they think it right journalists should receive. Rioters, on the other hand, comprise a crowd of people which has come together perhaps for this occasion only, and which has only the most rudimentary organisation behind it. Inevitably it is easier for journalists to get information from the police than from any authoritative source among the civilians, and this factor often is reflected in the relative emphasis given to police statements about such events. Thus access to information subtly begins to weigh in establishing a point of view; and it does so without the journalists necessarily having any conscious desire to cover these events from a given point of view. The essential point for us is that the screen can only offer a partial view, and it does so almost invariably by taking up a point of view. Though not impossible, it is very rare for the screen to be occupied by two points of view in conflict with each other.

The old notion, then, that the camera opens up a window on the world is inadequate. But what can be substituted for it? Plainly to reverse the old formula and advance the notion 'the camera *always* lies' is no more helpful, except that it reminds us that the camera always shows us something that is not there. This in itself, however, is worth considering, for what presents itself to the eye from the screen is not the thing itself but a curiously life-like image which both recalls its counterpart in the real world because it resembles it, and at the same time differs from it. This quality of simultaneous likeness to and difference from the real world characterises both picture and sound in the cinematic image. Thus simple notions of the camera and microphone as either infallible truth tellers or unstoppable liars will not do. We need to look for a more subtle explanation of the effect of the film making process upon the world it deals with.

Mediation

Such an explanation is to be found in an understanding of the processes involved in conveying information from source to recipient: mediation. Mediation indicates an area of considerable importance to the study of both film and television. It embraces a number of concepts which centre on the idea that the camera (and the microphone) do not merely transmit to audiences the world as it is, without changes. On the contrary the equipment, the work of the film crew, and several other significant factors to be touched on below, all influence the way any given film shows the world with which it deals. Marshall McLuhan, who credited himself with being the first to recognise the manner of this influence, summarised it in the famous slogan 'The Medium is the Message'.* His idea is that the medium embodies the message in such a way that it becomes totally different from the way in which any other medium would present the same message. Appealing though the concept is, encapsulated by such a pithy slogan, it too proves inadequate – for if applied at its face value, it would be wholly impossible to render a work of one medium into another medium, to transfer, for example, novels to the cinema or television screen. None the less, the idea, stripped of McLuhan's deliberate exaggeration, contains a healthy seed of truth: as everyone knows who has seen a well-loved novel presented as a screen attraction, direct and precise translation from the novel to film is simply not possible. It is enough to consider two aspects of the differences between the two media to make this clear.

The Medium and the Message: the novel and film

In a novel the leading characters become known to the reader by a variety of means. These include the things they say and do, and the way the novelist describes them as appearing. On film the same characters might say and do the same things, but there would be no call for anyone to describe the way they look. Instead the actor or actress playing the role appears before the audience, and his or her looks and voice go a long way towards defining the character in the minds of the audience. This in itself has large implications for the way we see screen characters. You could imagine a Western (the same Western) in which with the identical script the hero was first played by Gary Cooper, then by John Wayne, and on a final occasion by Clint Eastwood. Even with the same words in their mouths, the characters would be different. But, with the novel, the work of the reader differs from that which the viewer of a film undertakes in recognising a character, because the reader does not have a photographic representation of an actor before him. No matter how detailed the novelist's character description, the reader has space to fill it out for himself. My idea of the girl Tess will differ from yours when we read Hardy's *Tess of the D'Urbervilles*; but if we watch Roman Polanski's screen version of the book (1981) we are both confronted with the lineaments of Natassia Kinski as Tess, and she provides us with almost all we need to form an idea of Tess as presented by this version.

*Marshall McLuhan, *The Medium is the Massage*, Penguin Books, Harmondsworth, 1967.

If at this point film seems to have the advantage in presenting characters, we must recognise that there are aspects of them which it finds hard to present as well as the novel. The novelist, adopting what is usually known as the convention of the omniscient narrator, has no difficulty in revealing what his character thinks. The convention is so well known that the writer does not have to explain how he knows his character's mind: he merely tells you what is in it. For the film maker, by contrast, reaching the private thought of a character poses real problems. If he has him speak his thoughts out loud it seems excessively theatrical. There are, of course, ways round this problem, but they are awkward – what the novel in this instance can do with ease the film has to struggle to copy.

The Medium and the Message: television and radio news

Each of these two media exerts pressure on the material it conveys. An obvious point of comparison is news coverage. Notably television news, simply because the medium is visual, has to give priority to reports with pictures, if all other things are equal. A report accompanied by film is more attractive to the editor than an item which relies entirely on the 'talking head' of an announcer sitting at a desk. The pressure for visual information in television news is so great that events that have no significant existence other than for television are created daily to satisfy this need. For instance, politicians arrive at meetings and sit around for a few moments without doing business so that television cameras can get the shots that will be transmitted with a voice-over account of the decisions the meeting reached.

By contrast radio still works faster than television, and can be slightly more up to the minute. It is also free to give less time to the events themselves and more time to interpretation of them. A television audience will expect, if riots have taken place, extensive film or videotaped reports of the street clashes. Radio can proceed from a comparatively brief account of those events to an extended analysis of, for instance, their causes.

Mediation is the Message

Rather, then, than accepting McLuhan's over-enthusiastic dictum 'The Medium is the Message', it seems better to modify it to take account of the kind of shifts of emphasis that have just been described. We might say that the medium *inflects* (that is bends or shapes in some relatively subtle way) the message. This Handbook deals with some of the ways film and television inflect the messages which they mediate. In particular, it deals with the ways in which film makers bring the technical properties of the medium to bear upon those messages. It is neither a practical manual, nor a technical study of cinema: it will not teach you how to set up a camera, nor how to edit a sound recording. Rather, it concentrates on the effects the film maker can obtain through the technical mastery of the medium. In the light of what we have said above, it might be claimed that it is not the medium but *mediation* that is the message. However, if the processes and determinants of mediation were to be scrutinised in their entirety, several aspects of the subject would require more attention than the scope of this Handbook can afford. None the less, it would be worth identifying some of these aspects in passing.

The role of the media in society would form a central part of a complete study of mediation. How the media influence social response to the matters covered by news and current affairs topics; how society's views are themselves reflected by the media; in what way light entertainment integrates with social values – these and many similar questions would require investigation. A full examination of the processes of mediation would also have to consider the economics of the industry. With television and radio it would give close attention to the question whether the ownership and control of the different branches of the media have consequences for the programmes they carry. In the case of film, the pressures of capital institutions are nowhere more clearly seen than in the production and distribution arms of the American film industry. A full study of cinema would have to concentrate in part on the ways business decisions, often made in response only to financial pressures, affect film production. To take a simple example, the power of the studios and their concern to recover their investment in a production are such that they limit the kind of film that is likely to get made. It is much simpler in Hollywood to get funding for a production which resembles closely other films that have recently made money than for a film which is inventive and original. This situation arises because the marketing departments of the major studios find it easier to sell to the public a film with a conventional format than something which may seem unfamiliar. A study of this aspect of cinema might also consider how it happened that the motion picture industries of a number of European countries managed, by contrast, to produce films of a relatively adventurous character from the late 1950s on.

Again no full examination of mediation would fail to deal with the way films, television, and radio programmes communicate meaning. The way in which thought can be sent via one of these media to a viewer or listener is a huge subject in its own right. It leads the student to consider the mechanisms by which communication is achieved through an interlaced web of codes which the viewer or listener has learnt to recognise.

The work of the film crew

This Handbook inevitably only touches on the aspects of mediation mentioned above, but its principal concern is the study of another aspect of mediation. This has sometimes been described as the work of the film director, but it is more accurate to say that we shall look at the work of the whole film crew. For if the director makes many (but by no means all) of the creative decisions, the crew has the responsibility for interpreting those decisions and bringing them to realisation. This they do through their control of the equipment in their charge. Thus a director may decide that he wants a scene to look cheerful and bright, and he tells his lighting cameraman so. It is the craftsmanship of this individual and his lighting crew that creates the look of the film, the image that achieves the effect the director requires.

The reasons for giving precedence to the work of the film crew in a study of cinema and television are not hard to find. The work of the crew affects every image and every sound that reaches the audience, yet at the same time the effects of what they do are largely unrecognised. Most cinema goers take the performers to be the only significant elements in cinema; and while most people do not know what skills they employ in giving a screen performance, many do have a confident knowledge of what a John Wayne, a Clint Eastwood or a Jane Fonda appear to stand for. But the work of the film crew is not generally understood even to this limited extent. Though every inch of film passes through their hands, and the finished product only sounds and looks the way it does because they have done certain things to it, that work, because its nature and importance is so widely ignored, remains to all intents and purposes invisible to most film goers. The advantage of learning to appreciate what the crew has contributed is that it makes it possible to begin to understand the ways the film making process works upon and inflects the world in front of the lens.

Since the filmic treatment of a subject passes through several stages (lighting, shooting, recording, editing, and so on) – and each of them can change the appearance or sound of the product that is being put together – it makes sense to follow these procedures step by step. To do so gives some idea of the opportunities that face the film maker, so that for any specific film it becomes possible to see not only what techniques have been brought into service, but also what techniques have been avoided. For at each stage of production a series of choices confront the crew, and if certain techniques are adopted, others necessarily cannot be employed at the same time: obviously, if the camera has been set up to take a long shot of an actor it cannot simultaneously have him in close-up. It can move in, as the shot runs, to close-up, or it can cut in to a close-up in the next shot; but at any given moment, one option excludes the other. Equally self-evident is the fact that if a certain sequence of shots is cut together rapidly, the editor forfeits the option of cutting that same sequence slowly. It is worth raising this simple point because it backs up the assertion that in examining the details of the film maker's craft we are looking at a set of variables. As these two examples suggest, each of the variable elements in itself will be easily enough understood once it is recognised and deliberately looked for in a film. The rich and exciting complexity of cinema arises from the fact that in any given moment not one or two, but a whole set of such variable elements combine. It is this sheer number of alternative methods of covering a scene that provides the film maker with the opportunity – through the controls he exercises – to affect the way the film looks and sounds. Since he can do that, he also has the power to shape to some extent the responses of his audiences to what they see.

An example will help to make this point and show how effective the shaping controls of the film maker can be as he uses the techniques of his craft. This will also let us develop some sense of the ways in which his freedom to adopt whatever stylistic convention he might wish are limited. Consider a simple scene: a child walks by night through the long corridors of an empty office building. Now let us think of just a few of the many ways in which this scene might be filmed, noticing as we go along how they change its impact. In each case the child and the building are unchanged, though the various ways of covering them will make for considerable changes in their appearance.

1.   (*a*) The corridors are brilliantly lit.
     (*b*) The corridors are very dark, but little pools of light reach the walls from street lamps outside.

There are of course many other ways such a scene could be lit, but even so the effect here differs strikingly. In the first variant, everything can be seen with complete clarity. The fact that there is nothing to be looked at other than the harsh white walls emphasises the loneliness of the child. In the second version of the scene, the deep shadows conceal the child until it steps into one of the pools of light. But if they conceal the child, these shadows can also hide other creatures. No accident, then, that this style of lighting would be very suitable if the film crew wished to build a feeling of fear either of the unknown or of an attacker.

2.   (*a*) The camera remains motionless at the end of a corridor, and the child walks towards it.
     (*b*) With the camera in the same position the child walks away.
     (*c*) The camera moves along, close to the child.

Once again the scene could be covered in many other ways, and we shall investigate a number of them in Part 3. Of the alternatives suggested here, the first gives an *objective* view. Here the camera stands and looks on like a bystander. Neither in this nor the second alternative does it get involved in any way with the action. It merely observes. In the first version the approach of the child causes its image to take up an increasingly large area of the screen. This fact in turn tends to concentrate our attention on the child. The film maker can use this concentration on the child as the occasion to reveal something about it: perhaps as its face becomes visible in detail it will be seen to bear the marks of some emotion. Conversely in the second treatment of the scene, as the child walks away from camera, its image shrinks in the frame and leaves us looking once again at the walls of the long corridor; such a shot might emphasise its loneliness.

In the third instance, where the camera tracks with the child, the viewer seems to be moving along with it, which can in turn give rise to a feeling of sharing the actor's experience. Shots which have this effect are called *subjective*. The viewer, far from being a detached observer, is put in a position in which he enjoys the pleasurable illusion that the things that happen to the actor also happen to him. It is an illusion that pleases because, all the while, the spectator knows quite well that he sits in perfect safety in his seat.

With equal boldness, changes in the presentation of sound alter the impact of the scene. Again a multitude of ways of dubbing and mixing sound offer themselves to the film maker, so here are three possible ways of adding sound to our scene which do no more than hint at the possibilities.

3.   (*a*) The child walks almost silently. From beyond the walls of the building comes the sound of the last traffic of the night.

     (*b*) The child's footsteps are loud, and echo slightly as it walks through the corridors. Occasionally unexpected sounds leak out from the unseen offices and break the complete silence – a fan whirs on in one room, a draught causes a door to creak, and something like a footfall makes itself heard from behind another.

     (*c*) As the child wanders along, music becomes increasingly loud and from its association with an earlier scene, it recalls a happier time in the child's life.

We have not yet touched upon one of the most constructive stages in the making of film, editing; but even from the very limited evidence presented here, it can be seen that a very wide range of stylistic options present themselves to the film maker. In practice, however, a number of restrictions impose themselves on any production. Some of them are obvious, some less so, but they do mean that the full range of variables that the film maker's craft can encompass are not available on every production. Perhaps the most obvious limitation can be caused by lack of equipment. Without the equipment needed to do a certain job, the crew simply have to think of an alternative way of doing what they had in mind. Let us assume, referring back to the scene with the lonely child, that the director wanted to use a real building and to film the darker version of the scene (1*b*) lit only by light coming from the streetlamps. He would be able to get that shot only if he could obtain a raw film stock sufficiently sensitive to record a clear image in extremely low light levels. If he cannot get hold of such a stock, the director has to 'cheat' by creating the effect he wants with powerful film lights so that the film stock he can get records an image that looks like the scene he imagined.

The technical potential of film and television production equipment is today extraordinarily sophisticated. It is, of course, still possible for a crew to find itself faced with a task for which the necessary equipment does not exist, but another problem is more common: inadequate production funds to cover the hire of ideal equipment. Indeed in a whole number of ways production costs limit the freedom of the director to work in the way he chooses.

Probably the most expensive proposal for filming the child in the corridor – in terms of equipment – is 2*c*, which involves shooting with a moving camera. For this the crew would probably want to mount the camera on a dolly – that is, a small handpushed tracking vehicle – in order to obtain a smooth movement. If the production company does not own and cannot afford to hire a dolly, plainly it will have to cover the scene in some other way. But this can mean a change whose impact on the screen image is likely to be quite radical. Either the shot will be taken with a handheld camera, which because the image shifts with the movements of the operator's body provides the viewer with a different experience from the tracking shot; or the crew must shoot from a fixed camera position, which makes subjectivity much more difficult to achieve, and that was the whole point of shooting the scene this way.

Cash limitations have another equally serious effect upon the technical sophistication of a movie. For the production company has not only to buy stock and hire equipment, it has to pay the people who work on the film. In fact salaries and wages usually make up the biggest single item of cost in the budget of a film or television production. The longer technicians work or the longer a job takes to do, the more it is likely to cost. Thus certain ways of making a film will not be open to the director simply because they cost too much in staff time. Of the methods of shooting the scene with the child, that with the moving camera (2*c*) would cost most on these grounds. The intricacy of the shot is such that it would require careful rehearsal and planning so that all the technicians and the child moved together, pushing camera, lights, and sound recording equipment before them as the scene runs. A single shot of this kind can take hours to prepare.

The audience

An important additional factor which should be mentioned before we begin a detailed examination of the capabilities of the film maker's craft is the audience itself. In a society organised round a capitalist economy, a production company cannot continue indefinitely in business if its films lose money. Indeed, as has been mentioned, substantial parts of the film and television industries (and virtually all of them in America) run as a business first and foremost. The desire to communicate thought or drama with anything other than the most commercial appeal is remote from the primary objectives of such companies. Film makers working within the commercial system will want their movies to entertain, excite, or amuse, but above all to attract a big audience. To this end they prefer to make their films easy to understand. One of the chief methods of doing so is to make them recognisable by building them around elements familiar to film goers through long usage in other movies – the conventions of film making. In practice this means that commercial movies often fall into large classes, or genres. Westerns, gangster movies, and musicals are examples of genres in which individual films bear strong resemblances to other members of the class while at the same time inevitably featuring new and distinctive elements (a slightly different story, unfamiliar actors, or different character types, for example).

Whether the film is to belong to mainstream commercial cinema or is to be innovative and fresh, it will use filmic conventions to make itself understood. Film makers organise their filmic style according to conventions, just as in the case of the genres they may organise their stories to fit established pre-conceptions. In other words they may deliberately sacrifice their freedom to give their film whatever appearance they please in order to make it look like other films with similar characteristics. This is easily illustrated by the scene with a child in an office building. Although a director of that scene could make it in many different ways using no more than the limited alternatives we described, he could, if he wished to create an atmosphere of menace round the child, employ well established and extremely strong convention by combining certain of those alternatives. He would arrange his lights to create an image of a dark corridor with light scattered in small pools (1b); he would record the child's loud footsteps, and worrying noises in the unseen offices (3b); and he would combine these elements with one of two camera positions to place the audience in a classical situation of suspense which has hints about it that something horrific is about to happen. How that horrid event will strike the audience will now depend on the way the camera is used. If the director selects the option which has the camera placed unmoving at the end of the corridor with the child walking towards it (2a), the audience will experience the gathering expectation that something nasty will happen, probably as the child gets close up so that its reaction can be seen all too clearly. Of course if the audience already knows where an attacker is concealed, this shot gives it the unpleasant prospect of watching the child meander closer to certain danger. If the director chooses to cover this scene with the moving camera in the way we described (2c), not only does the audience have the chance to enter a subjective relationship with the child – that is, to feel closely attached to the child – it also cannot see much more than the child. Thus it will suffer a moment of shock at the same time as the child does, and it will have no more idea when this shock is to explode upon them than does the child. The point about both these ways of handling this scene is that they fit squarely into long established patterns of the suspense and horror movie. Though the director surrenders some of his creative freedom by adopting these expressive conventions, he sets his film in a context in which its intentions can hardly be mistaken by any viewer with experience of the cinema. So, here too, there is choice between innovation and established convention.

A narrative film, in creating a fiction with its own particular style, may employ new patterns of expression which require an audience to struggle in order to gain an understanding of *the way* things are stated so that it can begin to grasp *what* is being communicated. Alternatively it may opt to work as closely as possible with conventions of expression that have long familiarity through countless exposures to the audience. Either way, in any given scene the demands of style will render appropriate only certain of the choices available to a film crew.

We turn now to look in detail at the range of choices available to the film maker in the organising of his style. For the most part we shall do so as if the restraints we have just described – those caused by the requirements of finance, audience appeal and aesthetic convention – did not apply. In short we shall concentrate on what is technically feasible.

Part 2

Light and colour

IN THE BEGINNING (in cinema) there is light.* The word 'film' actually refers to a light-sensitive emulsion of chemicals whose response to light can be controlled in a precisely predictable manner. It is activated in the camera by exposure to carefully measured intensities of light, when the constitution of the chemicals undergoes certain changes. After laboratory processing of the exposed film stock, the latent image that light has imprinted in the emulsion emerges to the eye. Except in the case of certain special effects, we can say that without exposure to light no image will appear on film.

It is the work of a technical handbook, rather than of an analytical text of this kind, to describe how a cameraman determines the proper measure of light to which any specific film stock should be exposed. Later we shall refer to some of the principal characteristics of raw film stock as a means of showing how an image may be controlled by the selection of certain stock. For our present purposes it is convenient to begin with an account of ways of analysing the deployment of the sources of that light which, reflected from objects and actors, will eventually enter the lens of the camera.

Visibility of the subject

Because those areas of the image that are lit can be more readily scrutinised, the eye tends to look first at the brighter parts of a picture, and thereafter at the rest. This fact will help the lighting crew to decide how to set their lights, for, needless to say, their work amounts to more than simply making visible that which the spectator will look at on screen.

Four factors need to be considered:

1. The brilliance or *key* of the light
2. The *hardness* or intensity of the beam
3. The *contrast* or range of tones from darkest to brightest
4. The *position* and angle of the lights in relation both to the objects they illuminate and the camera.

These four variables bring about the main differences that can be

*With some aspects of television things may be different: television images can for certain purposes, be generated electronically.

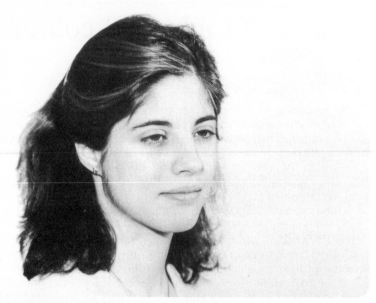

PLATE 1. High key image.

PLATE 2. Low key image, with high contrast.

achieved through the control of lighting and film stock. We will examine how they can be made to change the appearance of an image.

1. The lighting key

The expression 'lighting key' is open to some confusion since the main light in any set-up is known as the *key light*. However, the two should not be confused. The term 'key light' calls to mind its function, for this is the light that provides the key to the lighting of a scene. We shall see how important it is when we come to look at the placing of the lights.

The 'lighting key' is a more general term referring to the overall brilliance of the picture (which, of course, the key light establishes). The image can be either bright or dark; the phrase *high key* describes one which is bright, while *low key* refers to a picture that is relatively dark. It is also possible to refer to high or low key areas within a single image. However, the concept of the lighting key extends beyond the single image, and beyond the isolated shot. Since a shot usually forms part of a scene – and often a constant level of light will be maintained throughout – one can refer to the key of a scene. Indeed entire films can properly be described as either high or low key if they have a particular brilliance throughout. The films directed by Michelangelo Antonioni, or the celebrated glamorous movies coming from MGM (Metro Goldwyn Mayer) in the 1930s (so expensively dressed that they had to be well lit so that their lavishness could be appreciated), provide us with good examples of high key films, their images often shimmering with light.

In this way, the idea of the key has a further extension which illustrates how the way a film looks and the way audiences react to it are linked: the key of a film's lighting can also provide a clue to its mood. The classic example of mood set by low key imagery is provided by the American gangster movies of the 1940s, known as *films noirs* (literally, 'black films'). The notion of blackness refers both to the darkness of the picture and to the gloomy pessimism they often portray (typically they present characters living trapped, sickly lives in grim city surroundings). Thus a low key film may well deal with a grim, sad, or pessimistic subject. Conversely a high key film may have a happier subject, and an altogether more cheerful mood. It is, for instance, hard to think of a comedy (unless it happens to be a parody or take-off of a low key type of film) made in anything other than a relatively high key.

At this point we would do well to remember that we are not describing rules. We are, rather, discovering conventions, or codes of film making which have been exploited so often that they have become familiar. Such codes may be arbitrary and may have arisen from an experiment by one film maker that subsequently attracted a number of imitators. Other codes may derive from ideas and attitudes which are commonplace within the culture of a film maker and his audience. The associations of darkness with gloom and despair are so familiar to anyone who grows up in a Western culture that a film maker has no need to explain them. Light and gladness have equally strong connections in Europe – perhaps they derive from Northern gratitude for the sight of the sun through the clouds. But, however strong these associations, they do not force the film maker into adopting them. The conventions can be broken or ignored; and new conventional patterns can emerge which do not necessarily have connections with the old ones.

Antonioni's films, which have been mentioned as examples of high key work, help to make this point. His films could not possibly be thought of as presenting an optimistic view of the world; yet the images, whether in black and white or in colour, spill over with light. Obviously in responding to the mood of a film we react to more than just the key of the light. Antonioni's films (to say nothing of their bleak plots) combine high key with hard, flat light. Isolated in this unrelieved brilliance, his characters are locked into a brutal and chilling world.

A further point needs to be emphasised: an image is not necessarily exposed at an even key throughout. One part, the close-up of an actor's head perhaps, may be brightly lit, whereas the rest of the image, say the room in which he stands, may be quite dark. While in general terms it might be reasonable (if the whole scene takes place in a dark room) to describe this as a low key scene, a more precise account of this image is possible. One could refer to the specific areas of high and low key, speak perhaps of the contrast between them, and decide what was the dominant key of the image. In the example before us we have an image the dominant key of which is very low, but in which high contrast obtains between the low and high key areas.

2. The intensity or hardness of light

The simplest way to tell whether a light casts a hard or soft beam is to check the shadows. A narrow, intense beam in which the rays travel almost parallel to each other produces a hard light. Objects standing in such a beam tend to have a brilliant, clean, and sharp-edged appearance, and throw a hard-edged shadow. By contrast a broader and more diffuse beam in which light hits the subject with a less sharp edge, produces a soft light. Such a light softens the outline of objects and creates shadows that are not so deep and clean-edged. The harder the light, the higher the contrast ratio tends to be, and conversely, a softer light tends to reduce contrast (see below).

The intensity of a light is easily adjusted. Many movie lamps have focussing devices. Focussed, the lamp produces a hard light; unfocussed it emits a broader, softer light. Lighting crews carry diffusers, sheets of either fibre glass or other translucent material. Placed in the light path, these devices soften the beam.

Just as the key of an image can provide a visual metaphor for the director's intentions, so too can its degree of hardness. Again we are dealing with conventions – practised ways of doing things – rather than rules. None the less, softer lighting is often found in films whose subject, whether joyful or sad, is romantic – where a softer mood is to be evoked; and although hard lighting is used in a multitude of circumstances, it is a rare thing to find a thriller or a Western made in any other kind of light. The showy masculinity of heroes and villains alike would be lost in a Western lit with diffuse radiance.

3. The contrast ratio

The contrast ratio of an image refers to the range of tones between its darkest and brightest areas. In a high contrast image, the black areas of the image will be reproduced as very nearly black, and the brightest parts will be noticeably brilliant. By comparison a low contrast image reproduces a narrower scale of tones, perhaps limited to darker and lighter greys at the extremes.

High contrast photography
A high contrast image renders a marvellously sumptuous visual experience. Not only does the film reproduce a wide range of tones, but it does so in great detail. In black and white film high contrast produces a subtle variety of greys with precision, as well as registering the extremes of black and white. In colour, high contrast stock offers the cameraman a broad palette, again a wide range from dark to bright, and the opportunity to record saturated, bold colours.

Ideal for photographing confident, unambiguous images where black is black and white is white, the high contrast image has long been associated with Hollywood productions. There is a good historical reason for this connection, one which makes the spectator think of the high contrast image as the costliest and most glamorous, and which in turn ensures its continued use for productions of that kind. Originally the studios wanted to create high contrast photography because it gave more detail and a richer texture to the image. It turned out to be an ambition difficult and expensive to achieve. We have already mentioned that a harder, more intense beam tends to increase contrast. It does so because light falls with great intensity on illuminated areas, while the cut-off into shadows is razor-edged. A softer beam, on the other hand, allows light to spill into the shadows to some extent, and falls with less intensity on the lit areas. The provision of hard light required the focussing of the beam, and this development – via a simple lens – was

PLATES 3 AND 4. A high and low contrast rendering of the same face. The change in contrast has been brought about by altering the balance of light falling on the subject.

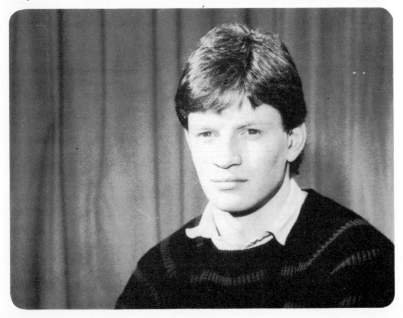

probably the cheapest item in perfecting high contrast cinematography. However, substantially higher levels of illumination were required for high contrast photography than for low contrast photography. This called not only for more lights and more power, but also for more members of the crew to spend longer hours to set them up, an expense which recurred for each high contrast production. Finally, a considerable amount of time and a great deal of effort was expended in perfecting film stocks that would take a high contrast image.

As a somewhat more expensive way of shooting film, high contrast cinematography tended to be used on the glossier studio productions which had the larger budgets. Thus were derived its associations – through the 1930s and 1940s in black and white and on into the 1950s with high contrast Technicolor – with glamour.

Low contrast photography
Low contrast cinematography encompasses a narrower range of tones and has different characteristics and associations. Noticeably it does not reproduce anything close to a perfect black; and low contrast colour film may not offer the full saturation (see page 44) of tones achieved with high contrast stock. The history of use of this kind of stock has also left associations which film makers sometimes still revive in their work to this day.

Low contrast film stock for a long while had the advantage that it was significantly *faster* than high contrast stock. In other words the emulsion on the former kind accepted light more rapidly than that on the latter. As we have already seen, one consequence was that high contrast stock required a high level of illumination. Altogether more adaptable, and needing comparatively low levels of illumination, low contrast stock suited not only the cheaper studio productions, but also circumstances where it was difficult to bring a battery of lights into action – in particular in newsreel production. Indeed, low contrast fast stock was so extensively used in the shooting of newsreels that it became for a long time associated with those films. Directors who wanted to make realistic dramas realised that if they filmed in low contrast black and white stock, they could give their work an appearance which the audience would associate with newsreel cinematography. Add to this the factor that the lack of expensive lighting gave the look of a less glossy production, and this method of working could convey to an audience the notion that the film makers were close to their subject in the way a studio crew could not be. It was no accident, then, that not only documentarists, but those who made feature films which took as their subject the lives of working people often chose low contrast black and white stock. The work of the Italian neo-realists immediately after the Second World War provides a number of examples. Although today's younger audiences cannot make the direct connection with newsreels of the 1930s and 1940s, the convention survives, and films made outside the big studios and portraying the lives of ordinary people often still appear with the same low contrast look to them.

In colour some of the faster stocks produce a low contrast image. From the early 1960s a visual style became fashionable in Europe which linked low contrast with high key, diffuse lighting. It was often used to give a cheerful, glowing look to the films. Sometimes this look reflected the atmosphere of the plot; but in other very striking instances (such as Victor Erice's *Spirit of the Beehive*, 1973, and Agnes Varda's *Le Bonheur*, 1965) the delicious appearance of the worlds that were represented proved an ironic contrast to inescapable troubles of the characters concerned.

Contrast ratio in television
Television receivers cannot yet carry images with the full contrast ratio rendered by a high contrast film production. Some loss of quality occurs when such a film is transmitted for television. The loss is worse with black and white film, which can render a much higher contrast than colour film. In either format the dark areas, which in the original could well have been filled with significant detail, become undifferentiated masses which the eye cannot penetrate.

4. Positioning of the lights

In practice a number of lights will usually be employed to illuminate a scene, and we shall describe various set-ups as we go on. Let us begin by assuming that we have only the *key light*, and that its beam is directed at a human head. As the light is moved from place to place astonishing changes occur to the image of that head. The actor throughout remains passive, looking directly at the camera – indeed a sculpted model of the human head would serve as well for this exercise, and that fact proves that the light rather than an actor's performance contrives these effects.

Front lighting
The key light stands close to the camera, and is directed on the actor's face from the front. Since the camera's lens and the light source are on almost the identical axis, any shadows cast by the light are all but invisible to the camera. (This incidentally is the case with most amateur flashlight photography in the home.) The face is fully and relatively evenly illuminated and, lacking shadows, appears flat or even squashed. None of the features stands out from the others except in so far as its colour or texture varies slightly from one feature to the next. With black and white cinematography, full frontal light of this kind creates a flat image in which variation arises only from the different intensities with which the various parts of the face reflect light back at the lens.

PLATE 5. Key light to the front, almost on the camera axis.

This first example of the placing of a single light source demonstrates that – crucially with black and white photography – the shaping of an image depends heavily upon the moulding effect of shadows. This is a function of light to which the lighting crew is very alert.

Backlighting
In this instance the light stands directly behind the actor's head. Now the effect achieved is almost the observe of the frontal position. Whereas in that case almost all the light from the source fell on the face, on this occasion scarcely any reaches the camera lens. The head is seen in silhouette, the face remaining in darkness. A rim of light illuminates the hair, the back of the neck, and the shoulders.

Plainly on its own this method of lighting will serve only specially heightened moments in a screenplay. But backlighting is often used in conjunction with other lights to achieve certain effects in black and white close-up work, and these will be described later (see page 32).

Sidelighting
Light falls on the head from a position to the side, at an angle of ninety degrees to the line of sight from the camera. It illuminates one side of the face and leaves the other in darkness. Where only one light is used, the division between the two halves will be very stark, and if it suits the

PLATE 6. Backlighting creating a rim.

PLATE 7. Lighting from the side at 90°.

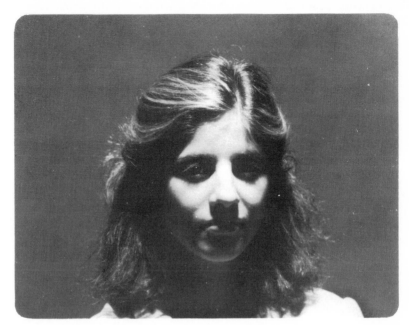

PLATE 8. Overhead lighting.

narrative, may suggest that only part of this character can be seen, while part remains invisible. In this case lighting would have helped to create a visual metaphor for a psychological type, the divided character.

It is unusual to light only from one source, and a variant of this image exists in which a second, dimmer light (called the *fill*, see page 29) gives a little light to the other side of the face. The actor may have a different expression on that side from the brighter half, and if so a similar metaphor to the first may be created.

Overhead lighting

If the lamp is placed above or below the head, it causes dramatic variations. These are seen at their most stark when it is directly over or underneath the head.

With the light source above the head, heavy shadows form in the eye sockets, below the nose, and under the chin. The effect can be sinister because, though the face is visible, the eyes remain concealed. This matters not only because actors make expressive use of their eyes in performance, but in particular because in Hollywood conventions what the actor expresses through his eyes often reveals the truth or falsity of the rest of the character's expression. A villain may smile with brilliant teeth at his victim, but his hard, unsmiling eyes declare to the audience his true, cold nature. Given that the eyes have this truth-revealing

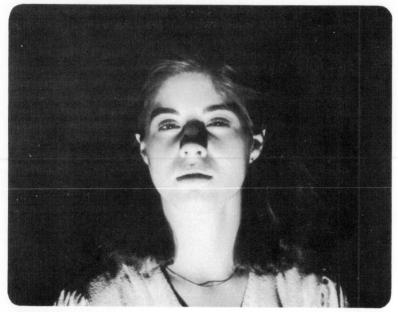

PLATE 9. Bottom lighting.

function, where they are kept in darkness, the audience finds the character unknowable at best, or reluctant to reveal himself, and therefore sinister at worst.

Lighting from below

This position reverses all the expectations of the audience about the way a face should look. The viewer is used to light descending. Now, hideously, shadows climb up the face. The chin and nostril are the most brightly lit areas, the cheek bones throw their shadows up into the eyes, and the forehead is obscure. Because its reversal of the familiar disorients the viewer, this lighting position occurs most often in horror films, where it has embellished all manner of ghouls, monsters and fiends.

A standard key light position

There is no single place that the key light has to be, and indeed it can occupy any of the positions, or points between the positions described above. For close-up lighting where no particular point is being made about the character or his circumstances, the key light will probably be placed somewhere on an arc between the camera and a point 45° to either side of it. It will either be level with the subject, or a little higher. Thus one side of the face will be lit more fully than the other, and there may be shadows on the side away from the light in the eye socket, and thrown by the nose. If the lighting is too severe these shadows may 'scar' the face; softened, they help mould the face. It is the *fill light* that softens these harsh shadows.

The fill light

Lighting from a single position, though dramatic, is uncommon because it lacks subtlety. Its subjects are either lit or in shadow. The fill light is the first means of introducing half light between the extremes.

Once again its name describes its function. This light fills out the image created by the key. In the close-up images just described, the fill would be directed at another part of the face (usually the other side) from that lit by the key. It lights the face with lesser intensity than the key, and with a more diffuse beam. Thus its effect is to soften the harsh shadows cast by the key and to mould the contours of the face with a more subtle blend of light and darkness than the key can render unaided.

The simplest demonstration of key and fill working together occurs when a television crew record an interview for a news or current affairs programme. Because they have to work fast and in restricted locations where (as in an executive's office, for instance) they are expected to make as little disturbance as possible, they will be equipped only with a few lightweight lamps. Even in relatively formal interviews the crew would be unlikely to use more than three lamps, very often making do with two. Where three lamps are used, two will be mounted in the same position and will provide the key, the third being the fill. Where only two identical lamps are in service, the one which acts as fill is set further from the subject than the key, and its beam is softened. In such circumstances the key light would commonly be placed at about 45° to one side of the camera axis, and slightly above the subject. The fill would stand at much the same angle on the other side of the axis, probably further away from the subject. This positioning has the advantage that it keeps the lights well clear of the interviewer and crew and lets them move about fairly freely.

Adequate for current affairs and news television, where what the interviewee says rather than the way he appears matters, such a lighting pattern would be rather crude for the more studied art of feature film production. There the fill and key would not normally be placed in such total symmetry, for fear of creating double shadows, especially from the nose. If one light is close to the camera, the other will tend to be at more of an angle. If the key is placed at a point about 45° from the camera and the fill stands close to the camera, shadows will be created only by the former, and pleasantly softened by the latter. It is not uncommon in feature film production for more than one fill light to be directed onto the face. In order, for example, to reduce the weight of the face and suit it to a certain kind of romantic vision an additional fill might be aimed at the lower part of the face to lighten the shadows under the chin.

PLATE 10. Key and fill lights: key at 45° left, fill on camera axis.

PLATE 11. Key at 30° left, fill on camera axis.

PLATE 12. Key at 15° left, fill on camera axis.

PLATE 13. Key at 45° left, fill at 30° right.

A standard three-light set-up

Lighting requirements for colour and black and white film differ. With colour it will often suffice to use no more than key and fill lights. This is so because colour provides the viewer with one more system of reference than monochrome (black and white) film. The eye can distinguish one shade of colour from another readily enough. But in monochrome certain true colours are reduced to identical tones of grey or black on screen. If a dark-haired individual stands in front of a dark wall, the eye, and colour film, have no difficulty in distinguishing the person from the wall. In monochrome, however, the hair may look too much like the background for the outline of the head to emerge clearly. Thus backlighting is almost indispensible in black and white photography. And even in colour it may be used for the same end, to make the actor stand out from the background.

The backlight does this, as we have seen (page 25) by rimming with light the whole or part of the head. Often the backlight is placed both above and behind the actor, and picks out just the top of the head. In effect the backlight provides an edge to the image of the player. There is of course no obligation on a film maker to deploy this device any more than any other. Where it is absent, the monochrome image has a certain flatness (that is the three dimensional appearance of the image tends to be markedly reduced). A film maker may well think this rather muted effect suits his screenplay, and he may deliberately choose it. It might, for instance, be created for a socially conscious drama about working people in which the director particularly did not want to glamorise their surroundings.

The key, fill, and back lights are the three basic positions for close-up photography. There can, of course, be more. The classic style of Hollywood portrait cinematography, for instance, required light to be visible in the eye of the actor. This was contrived by tiny spotlights, sometimes called 'inky dinkies', aimed at the eyes from close in to place a spark of light in the pupil.

Not only can additional lights be used, but those three can themselves be moved so far from their familiar positions that they become all but unrecognisable. In *film noir* (see page 19) the key light may be moved so far round to the side of, or even behind the characters that it becomes known as the 'kick light'.* Alternatively it may be right overhead, or let light fall onto only a fragment of the face. Typically the fill light will be very weak, and backlighting is either absent or so intense as to look garish. Their whole lighting pattern contributes a lot to the melancholy and oppressive look of these films.

Finally, although we have for the most part spoken as though there

*J. A. Place and L. S. Peterson, 'Some Visual Motifs of Film Noir', *Film Comment* (10,i) January 1974, 30–5.

PLATES 14 AND 15. The same close-up, first without, and then with highlights in the eyes.

were only one lamp in each position, this is by no means always the case. A battery of lights may in certain circumstances be mounted in each position, either to intensify the beam, to broaden it, or even to mix hard with soft light. This is more likely to be the case when a character has to move.

Movement

We have been discussing lighting as if the actor were rooted to a single spot; but the whole point of film is that it is an art of movement. So what happens to the lights when the actor walks about? It goes without saying that he will move into darkness unless something is done. The two methods of dealing with the problem are logical enough. Either the lights move with the actor, or the actor moves along a planned 'route' which has been lit in advance with fixed lamps.

Travelling lamps

To move all the lamps required for the more intricate set-ups described for close-ups would be a cumbersome business; and it would be virtually impossible to keep them all directed with precision upon a walking actor. Fortunately it is not necessary to proceed in this way because the mind of the viewer requires different information when an actor moves. There is no longer time to scrutinise the face in detail, as was possible when the actor was in stationary close-up; and now the viewer wants to know more about the movement itself than about the expression on the actor's face. The mind busies itself with such problems as finding out what the character is doing, and why. Thus the kind of precise lighting that can be obtained for static shots is not called for when actors move. Accordingly a typical arrangement is for the actor in movement to be covered by massive floodlights, called 'brutes', which can be rolled along by the lighting crew as the camera and cast shift about. Such an arrangement provides constant and even light on the players, though it sacrifices the moulding of detail.

Static lamps

It may be easier, particularly if the camera itself is not to move, or if a scene is being shot in a confined space, to have the actor move through a number of lighting positions. Typically lights would be set with precision for those points at which the performer was to pause, and, in particular, where such points are to be close to the camera. Elsewhere, however, his path would be lit by floods where light was required. This method has the advantage that the crew can choose either to light the actor to a relatively constant level as he roams around, or to have him move through variable fields of light and dark. A further variation can be achieved if an actor is lit by static lamps while he stands still, but by travelling lamps as he moves.

Lighting the set

We now have a working account of some of the things that lights can do with performers, but as yet our set or location is a visual mess. The light that spills off the characters does not suffice to illuminate their surroundings, and the actors cast heavy multiple shadows if we leave things as they are. It follows, of course, that the first two functions of set lighting have already been identified: to light the set itself and to eliminate or at least reduce the number of shadows cast by players. The second task is achieved by lighting areas where unwanted shadows fall to a level that blends in with the rest of the set. Where a set has been lit in this way evidence of it can be seen in the general brightness that suffuses the set behind the players, and which can add a sense of heightened glamour to the scene.

Illuminating a set, then, does more than merely bathe it in light. But it does do that too, and the film maker has a choice of the levels of brilliance that he will use to reveal his set: whether it should be equally bright throughout, and whether it should be in the same or a different key from the characters. Considerations of cost as well as of artistic intent come into play here. Not only does it cost more to rig the greater number of lights needed for high key work, but the set, since it will be seen with greater clarity, has to be made in much closer detail. At one time, in the late 1920s and early 30s, Warner Brothers exploited a device which both looked good for the kind of movie they were making and saved them money, and many have imitated them since: in their popular gangster movies of that era they left the sets very dark indeed. The gloom matched the dark mood of the movies, and the saving in costs contributed to a cost-cutting programme which made the studio one of the more efficient of that time.

Practical lights

Practical lights tend to confuse students who are learning the elements of screen analysis. They are those lights that are part of a set and appear on screen. In this they differ from the movie lights that have been described, which the crew take pains to conceal. It is tempting to assume that the lamp that can be seen is the source of light on the set and on the faces of the players. It is a temptation not the less enticing because the lighting crew, to give the impression of reality, may well light the set in just such a way that the practical lights appear to be the true sources. In actuality this is seldom the case. For a start practical lights do not have the output needed to register an image on most film stocks, and, furthermore, light from them would fall randomly on the subject. Careful examination of a scene usually reveals lighting effects which practical lights would not yield. The exception to this pattern is the work of the television documentarist operating with modern video technology in offices and shop floors. His equipment will respond to fluorescent light, and uneven shadows give the picture a roughness that audiences are willing to accept as appropriate to footage shot in real surroundings.

Flood and spotlights

In the lighting of either a set or an interior location both floods and spotlights may be called for. The floodlight has a very high output and will light a much wider arc than the spotlight. Thus it serves to illuminate sets which require an even and high-key light. On the other hand the spotlight, because it casts a narrower, more intense beam, tends to be useful where particular parts of a set are to be picked out. Precisely because it can be focussed more accurately, the spotlight is much used to light actors in the kind of circumstances we have already described.

Lighting and the third dimension

Among other things that can be achieved by the selective lighting of a set, it can add to or diminish the viewer's sense of depth 'into' the screen; that is, it can help persuade the viewer that the scene represented on the two-dimensional screen still has its third dimension. Alternatively it can reveal the scene, with high key light falling evenly across the image from the front, as relatively flat.

The kind of effect that can be created can be illustrated by two examples in which the lighting crew add to the sense of depth in the perceived image. The first applies a method of selective lighting, for if an area of the foreground and an area of the background are lit, but part of the middle ground should be left comparatively dark, then the eye of the observer constructs from what it sees the idea of depth between the two lit areas, that is of depth into the screen. Secondly, lighting the set from the side appears to increase perceived depth, as opposed to front lighting which reduces it.

Texture

The choice of how to position lights will also be influenced by decisions about the kind of textures surfaces should have. A surface looks

PLATE 16. Apparent depth between the foreground (the branches of the tree) and the background accentuated by two distinct planes of light and dark.

smoother when lit from in front than from the side. Under certain circumstances lights may be positioned along the edge of a surface – such as a wall, to make its rough brickwork stand out more clearly. Ultimately decisions as to whether this kind of detail is desirable depend upon the kind of atmosphere the film makers wish to create to fit with the action of a screenplay. While it would be an oversimplification to say that a specific texture will help establish a specific atmosphere, it seems reasonable to claim that a rough surface is more noticeable than a smooth one. In that case texturing may be a means by which a director can call attention to parts of a set in preference to others.

Atmosphere or mood

Clearly the way the set is illuminated helps set the atmosphere of a scene. An astonishing range of possibilities presents itself to the lighting crew, as we have begun to see. The viewer who momentarily forgets how rich these possibilities are can remind himself by looking at almost any scene and thinking about how he would have reacted to it if the lighting had been different. A scene shot in a hard, clear light will not only look different but will communicate a different atmosphere from a scene in which the same action is lit unevenly in pools of harsh light isolated in

PLATE 17. Close-up of a tree-trunk in direct sunlight. The bark appears deeper on the right, where light shines across the fissures, than on the left, where it shines into them.

enveloping darkness; and both these versions would feel different again from another covered in a soft, even radiance.

Actually we do in life respond to the light around us (lovers dim the lights, and by night dark passages frighten us); but usually there are around us many other demands on our attention. In cinema the light cast on the screen, and the sound coming from the speakers are the dominant preoccupations of our eyes and ears. The impact of a change in a lighting pattern is therefore all the greater, and we do not have to think about it to be affected by it.

Exteriors

Though it has not until now been an issue, we have, in describing a lighting system in which the crew have total control over the illumination of a scene, actually been concentrating on work done in interiors. Our unspoken assumption has been that no daylight intruded on the set. Whatever light fell on the subject did so because a technician had selected and rigged a lamp.

When by contrast we begin to consider the evaluation of outdoor light, it seems at first as if there can be nothing to say. Daylight is

PLATES 18 AND 19. Atmosphere created by different levels of light. Here the amount of light passing through the lens has been varied, but not the level of light falling on the subject.

PLATES 20 AND 21. The same scene in sunlight and on a cloudy day. Contrast decreases in the absence of direct light, and edges soften.

daylight – the crew shoot in the light available, and that is all there is to it. In actuality, as a closer examination of almost any outdoor scene reveals, the crew continue to exercise a measure of control over the light.

Time of day

Outdoor light varies constantly. A shot taken in the early morning, with the pale light slanting in will be very different from a shot in the brighter, vertical light of noon. A film crew which forgot that fact would make a very odd movie indeed, for one of the things they have to do is to ensure that the lighting in any given shot is well matched to the light in the next shot. In practice this means that a scene that takes place, for example, at midday has to be shot near to that time of day. When the sun moves on, completion of that scene has to be held over to the same time on a later day. From our standpoint as viewers, this is yet another piece of evidence that what we find on the screen is there deliberately. Of course, wonderful lighting effects can be obtained simply by shooting in unexpected hours of the day, particularly either early or late.

Weather

Weather changes affect natural light as drastically as the passing hours – and again in feature films we can be confident the crew will have tried to wait for the weather conditions they want before shooting. Even a simple and familiar cinematic episode like a chase will arouse very different responses if it is played out in bright daylight, or in the turmoil of a storm, or in misty evening light. The first version might do little other than centre on the relationship between pursuer and pursued; the second, in the storm, might be so set up as to encourage the viewer to reflect on the smallness of the characters' lives measured against the confused elements; and played out in mist, the same scene might develop a sense of unreality.

Control over exterior light

A well equipped crew making a feature film will usually go further than selecting the time of day and weather that best suit the story line and atmosphere of their production. They will want in one way or another to alter the available light, and they may do so in order to achieve one of a number of effects.

Reflectors
In broad day additional light may be brought to bear on a subject by reflectors. Their commonest employment is to provide a fill light against the brilliant key of direct sunlight. While cloud diffuses the sun's light,

on clear days sunlight produces sharp and deep shadows which can be softened by light bounced onto the subject from a reflector.

Alternatively reflectors can direct light to areas, in shade for example, where there is insufficient light to make good photography possible.

Artificial light outdoors

Whatever reflectors can do, artificial lights can do at least as well, if at greater expense. So it is not uncommon to find big flood lights ('brutes') directed at actors to soften shadows on their faces. Such shadows on film look more obtrusive than they do in life. In particular where characters (as in the Western) wear hats, light, whether from reflector or lamp, will be beamed up under the brim of the headwear to fill the whole face. If the crew wish to have the actors stand out from their surroundings, brutes may be shone on them no matter what the available light. This technique features often in Hollywood movies and contributes to the glamorising of actors. The effect of the extra light on the players (even though most members of the audience may never perceive it consciously) is to heighten their presence, to make them seem more vivid and more to the foreground than would have been the case if they had been lit evenly with the rest of the location.

If the unit has the lighting power, which again presumes considerable cash backing, this treatment can be extended to the setting itself. It is not uncommon for film units to enhance the attractions of a glowing exterior by, for instance, adding to the brilliance of the sun pouring through the leaves behind the heads of a pair of young lovers. If the scene looks unnaturally beautiful it is probably because it *is* unnatural.

Diffusers

If the light of the sun is bright, but unpleasantly harsh, a relatively cheap method of softening it for close ups and tight group shots can be arranged by having performers act under a gauze canopy. The camera operator keeps it out of frame so the audience is not aware of its presence, and the fabric diffuses the light.

These methods make it possible for a film crew to influence available daylight on location, and to organise many of the effects obtained on fully controlled sets. Once again we see that the way light falls on its subject will have been the result not of accident but of careful planning – planning which will have commenced at the scripting stage and have been followed through to the shooting.

Night scenes

The idea of exterior cinematography by night sounds like a contradiction in terms: no light, no image. None the less, scripts often call for such scenes, and there are two ways of going about shooting them, the results of which look quite distinctive to the viewer.

Increasingly rapid film stocks make the light that is available on well-lit city streets sufficient to render background detail. Light in the foreground is augmented, particularly where it falls on actors. This method is known as 'night-for-night' shooting, and it requires that every visible detail must be lit. On location there may be enough available street and advertising light to keep the picture interesting; by contrast, on the studio-built street set, the night scene must be created in its entirety by lighting every detail that the camera is to register. The crew have total control.

The alternative method, which costs less, is to shoot 'day-for-night'. The scene is filmed in daylight, usually in bright sunlight. A combination of underexposure (that is deliberately letting insufficient light reach the emulsion so that the image does not reach full brightness) and of filtering the light entering the camera makes for an effective simulation of night. This treatment usually produces a dream-like unreality which resembles a moonlit scene. Objects stand out with unnatural clarity, and everything from the foreground to the horizon is picked out vividly. Night-for-night shooting, however, produces a frame predominantly dark and in which the horizon cannot be seen.

To generalise, the night-for-night treatment may be said to suit urban dramas – gangster and police movies use it extensively. It adds to a claustrophobic, sombre feeling these movies often project. Day-for-night shooting, on the other hand, works satisfactorily in rural scenes, particularly those created for melodrama rather than realistic fiction. It is often found in the Western, where the heightened unreality it provides may add to the sense that the action is a mythic ritual of good and evil played out beyond the limits of daily time.

Colour

Almost everyone who prefers colour films to black and white justifies that preference by remarking that colour is 'natural'. In the sense that the world we live in is colourful this is an obvious truism. However, the contrary statement is closer to a more precise truth: that in fact colour in film is *never* natural, for it cannot present us with a perfect copy of the world it represents. It fails for two principal reasons: the characteristics of raw film stock, and the effect of the projected transparency.

The characteristics of raw film stock

With colour as with black and white we must recognise that what we see in the cinema depends upon what the stock will register. No stock registers colour without some degree of bias. Three factors may be noted:

Colour bias
The stock may register one or two colours more strongly than others. Blues and reds, for example, might be particularly well represented, while the greens might take on a blackish tinge.

Contrast
As we have already discovered (page 21) some stocks reproduce images with a higher contrast ratio than others.

Saturation
The strength or weakness of a colour is referred to as its saturation. Some stocks, for example those made by the old Technicolor processes, have the capacity to reproduce deeply saturated colours; others, like certain modern emulsions, are manufactured to render delicate and desaturated colours.

These variables are predictable, and cameramen and directors choose the stock that will give them the effects they want. The maker of a Western may well prefer to render his screenplay in high contrast, saturated colours (*Shane*, 1952, and *The Searchers*, 1956, are classic examples). On the other hand a film set in the 1930s may well be made in desaturated colour to gain the impression of the washed out colours fashionable in that decade.

The effect of the projected transparency

When an image is projected onto a screen, white light passes through the film and is coloured by the translucent emulsion on it. This process, though simple, makes the projected image look unnatural to the extent that it shines with a brilliance which makes the colours almost luminous. In the pre-cinematic world such a sight could only have been equalled by bright sunlight streaming through a stained glass window.

Actually this seemingly arbitrary link between an old form of luminous colour and a new one invites us to think of colour as it was once perceived, in order to learn something about the way we enjoy it today.

Colour and pleasure

Much of the colour by which we are surrounded (our clothes, cars, furnishings, and much more) is, of course, man-made. This density and intensity of colour in our lives is something quite new. Before durable and cheap dyes and paints had become widely available, European life was in the main, drab for all except the most wealthy. The excited celebrations of generations of poets, from the middle ages on through the centuries, of the richness and colour of spring provide indirect evidence of this fact. Exotic dyes were available, but only at a price the wealthy could afford. Because of the general drabness, a colourful street parade or a stained glass window would have been the object of fascinated attention. Aldous Huxley argues in *Heaven and Hell* (1956) that the parades of their followers dressed in gaudy costumes which the nobility organised from time to time would have added immensely to their stature. This would have been not only because of the wealth they displayed in so doing, but also as a consequence of the pleasure men derive from experiencing rich, saturated colours. It is so great that we tend always to be attracted to colourful things first, and then to drab ones.

Huxley goes further and makes the case for colour having special, virtually magical properties in the minds of many. He uses as evidence man's fascination with the brilliant iridescent images released in the mind by certain drugs. Now precisely because of their luminous quality, movie images have more in common with the purity of colour seen in dreams and visions than they do with reality. The almost magical attraction that film colour exerts reveals itself in the frequency with which people describe film as like a dream. It is not necessary to argue, of course, that film leads its spectators towards mystical experience. Even religions have never used colour as more than a trigger to release the mind from worldly problems, and they have always called for meditation to carry their devotees further – but the commercial cinema undoubtedly does both cause and rely on the pleasure of the spectator and the use of the special qualities of colour in film has much to do with that.

The uses of colour

Continuity

As with any other of the variables in the control of the crew (lighting, camera, sound), the relationship between one shot and another either establishes or breaks continuity. If two successive shots of what would otherwise appear to be the same scene have markedly different colour values the audience is likely to think either that there has been a mistake or that time has passed. So where it wishes story continuity to flow smoothly, the crew has to try to keep colour values constant. On the other hand a change of time or place (say from an exterior to an interior) may well be the occasion to change colour balance as a way of reinforcing the difference between the two scenes.

Atmosphere

Colour invariably affects the way an audience reacts to what it sees. This will be the case even where colour has been used carelessly, which often happened in early productions in the 1930s. Its impact is such that the makers of any professional feature film will in some way or other 'colour code' their picture. At the very least this will entail the careful selection of a film stock with an appropriate colour bias. More commonly colour coding will call for the preparation of sets and costumes so as to give predominance to certain colours at the expense of others. What is more, not only the pro-filmic material (the things in front of the camera), but also the filmic treatment will be colour biassed: lights may be tinted by gels, the light transmitted to the stock may be modulated by filters on the camera lens, and, most important of all, the stock itself may be subject to special processing in the laboratory to adjust its colour rendering.

It is not difficult to detect the colour bias of a film. If the bias is marked, it will be hard to miss. If there does not seem to be a bias, it is worth considering what colours are missing, or hardly seen at all, as well as what colours dominate. And there is a further method of testing this, going by the formal name 'commutation': it can be used in judging the operation of all the effects of cinema. All this involves is the mental substitution of an alternative effect for what is actually seen, in order to test one's response. If, for example, green predominates on the screen, imagine what the effect would be if red were substituted. If the consequences are drastic, the colour green is making a specific contribution to the meaning of the film at that point.

The Sting (1973) and *Chariots of Fire* (1981) provide us with convenient examples. Like a number of modern films they seek to create an atmosphere of a certain period, the 1920s and 1930s, and they draw on the effects of colour coding as one of the means by which to do so. Browns and sepias predominate; creams, greens, and heavily muted pinks, reds, and primrose tones also feature; but blue is seldom seen unless the sky happens to be in frame. Often, particularly with interiors, everything appears to be seen through a light sepia wash, which would be produced by filters and processing. It is not necessary to assume the 1920s and 1930s actually looked this way; in any case the vast bulk of the cinema audience is too young to have lived then. Rather, the careful tones and the sepia wash generate a vague sense of the era through associations we recall with old sepia tinted photographs. It is the association with the *image* rather than the *actuality* of the period which makes the film makers' tinting successful in this instance.

We can now revert to the idea of 'commutation' and check it by asking whether the viewer would have reacted differently to *The Sting* if its dominant colour had been a cold, hard blue. The answer has to be that it would have changed things very much. A cold blue (a tone that often dominates in the more sinister police movies of recent years) would have tended to make the audience feel alienated and apart from the action, would have nudged them into a hostile attitude towards the film's tricksters. As it is, the warm browns and harmonious muted reds and greens create a comfortable atmosphere which reassures the audience and helps persuade them to enjoy and sympathise with the confidence tricks of the witty rogues who are the film's heroes. Once again we find ourselves closer to dream than to reality.

Colour, however, can do more than generate feelings of warmth or coldness. A. J. Reynertson has described its powers well:

> The emotional effects of colour are well known. All human beings form associations with colours, and while the associations are not all identical, some associations tend to cluster around certain colours within any one culture. In Western society for instance, red tends to be associated with life, blood, vigour, love, violence; blue with coolness, placidity, valour, honesty, strength. Yellow is associated with sunshine, gaiety and cowardice; green with growing things, life, fertility; and purple with nobility and sacrifice.*

These associations, as Reynertson goes on to say, are suggestive. They have to match and complement nicely a mood which the director has to be sure to establish by other means than colour alone. And it goes without saying, of course, that colour can be used to work up associations quite contrary to those listed here, however well established they may be.

Colour symbolism

Besides its exclusively emotional, suggestive use, colour can be employed in a more precisely symbolic way, though even in this case its emotional impact will continue to be felt. For example, in *Don't Look Now* (1972), red provides a troubling link between events that seem to have no logical connection. The association is made by the repeated presentation to the audience of triangular shapes of red that usually stand out from their visual surroundings. These figures have considerable impact because they appear at worrying moments; but not having the information to judge their meaning, the audience has to puzzle over them until the end of the film when the problem is resolved. Thus in this instance colour symbolism calls the viewer into an active, questioning relation with what he sees.

Colour symbolism does not have to demand this much from the audience. *Electra Glide in Blue* (1973) contains several passages in which

*A. J. Reynertson, *The Work of the Film Director*, Focal Press, London, 1970, p.106.

changes in the entire colour bias of the film destroy any possible belief in realism. A sequence may begin in blues and slowly bleed to reds, or may reverse the process, red and blue being the dominant tones. With this film failure to undo the mystery does not stop the spectator from understanding the plot, but it does limit his appreciation of it. The two colours are in effect in opposition, the blue tones suggesting the uniforms of the police, to whose ranks the hero belongs. These blues are markedly cold, even brutal, and this feature is readily associated with the callous and improper behaviour of the men. Red, as we know, has certain inevitable ties to the idea of life and vitality, but also, conversely, blood and death. Thus it embodies formally the hero's attempts to free himself from the blue of the police mentality, and to become more fully human – an attempt which costs him his life in the end. In this film, then, colour takes a role which still relies on its suggestive powers, but has specifically symbolic values too.

Part 3

The camera

AS THE INSTRUMENT through which the moving image is registered, the camera affects that image. It does so in a number of ways which have their consequences for the way a spectator sees the pictures it relays.

Camera placing

It is not difficult to recognise that a camera can be placed either near to or distant from its subject. It follows that the positioning of the camera alters the information it relays about that subject.

The various positions have names which, while they do not precisely measure the placing of the camera, describe its relation to its subject effectively enough. There are two ways of thinking about the effects of these placings. One is to note the relative size in the frame of the subject (which as often as not will be a person). The other entails looking at the relative proportion of the subject to the background in the frame. We shall look at both factors.

Long shots

Extreme long shot (ELS)
In this type of shot the camera reaches its furthest distance from the subject, which as a consequence takes up a very small part of the frame. The setting dominates the picture. This shot is also known as the 'establishing shot' because it has a long history of use to establish or set the scene of a fresh piece of action. If the audience sees an establishing shot of a trail of horsemen winding its way across distant hills, it can hardly doubt what kind of film it opens.

Long shot (LS)
The camera remains distant, but not so far off. The setting continues to take up most of the space in the frame. A standing actor fits completely within the frame, neither his head nor his feet being cut off, though they are not far from the frame line (the outside edge of the picture frame).

Medium long shot (MLS)
The frame line now cuts off a small part of the subject, which is still at a moderate distance from the camera. In the case of a standing actor, the lower frame line traverses his calves, cutting off his feet and ankles.

PLATE 22. Extreme long shot.

PLATE 23. Long shot.

PLATE 24. Medium long shot.

PLATE 25. Medium close shot.

PLATE 26. Close-up.

PLATE 27. Extreme or big close-up.

In differing degrees all the long shots give most of the frame space to the setting of the actor or other subject. If the picture remains static much of the viewer's attention will be given to that larger area, to the setting; and unless an actor does something which significantly dramatises his character in some way (for instance by making a large movement or by speaking) the spectator will not pick up much information about him because he figures too small in the frame for a lot of detail to show. Costume and body attitude may be clear enough, but no more – and in the extreme long shot even these may be indistinct.

It follows that a film which works extensively in long shot may be more interested in the surroundings or environment of its characters than in their personalities. Social circumstances rather than the individual may be the centre of attention. Some documentaries with social themes tend to favour keeping people in the longer shots for that reason.

Medium shots

Medium shot or Mid-shot (MS)

In such a shot the subject or actor and its setting occupy roughly equal areas in the frame. About half the subject is excluded from the frame; in the case of the standing actor, the lower frame line passes through the waist.

Medium close shot (MCS)

The camera approaches the subject a little more, but though the actor or other subject now just dominates frame space, the setting can still be seen, though with slightly less emphasis than in the medium shot. The lower frame line now passes through the chest of the actor.

In these medium shot positions, frame space divides fairly evenly between the actor and his setting. The medium shot is also the classic angle for the tight presentation of two actors (the 'two-shot'), or with dexterity three (the 'three-shot'). It is, then, a shot in which the individual will be related with almost equal emphasis either to another person or to his environment. A certain amount of detail in the face of the character can now be seen, but the audience does not lose sight of his surroundings.

A film which restricts itself to long and medium shots may well have an interest in characters as types, but not as individuals with distinct psychological traits. It may wish to set characters in their society, showing them among their fellows and in the kind of milieu or background to which they belong. That is precisely what the Italian neo-realists of the 1940s and 1950s intended, showing the lives of working

PLATE 28. Academy or standard screen proportions: height to width ratio 1:1.3.

PLATE 29. Widescreen: height to width ratio 1:1.8.

PLATE 30. Cinemascope: height to width ratio 1:2.25 or more.

and poor people in war-damaged Italian cities. In Roberto Rossellini's *Rome, Open City* (1946) hardly a close-up is seen.

Close shots

Close-up (CU)
The camera stands so close to the actor that it obtains a head-and-shoulders shot. If an object is being filmed, it will occupy most of the frame. As its name implies, this shot allows the audience to scrutinise the primary subject in detail, and that subject now takes almost all the frame space.

Extreme or big close-up (ECU or BCU)
For this shot the camera comes so close that only a part of the face is seen, but that registers in enormous detail. There is room for nothing else on screen.

With the close shots the primary subject is seen in detail so intense that its nature is revealed virtually to the exclusion of information about anything else. In close-up, on a large screen, the emotions of an actor can overwhelm an audience. A tear may run two metres down a cheek; in extreme close-up a smile can fill the screen. Thus the close-up serves well to reveal the inner state of a character, because an expert actor can use his face as a means of expressing subtle inflections of emotion. In extreme close-up we seem almost to be inside the head of the actor. The intimacy is extraordinary because normally in life we do not get as close as that to anyone other than our lovers and members of our families.

Widescreen

The proportions referred to in the foregoing account of the various camera positions describe what happens in the standard screen (that is the screen of roughly the same proportions as the television screen). But the widescreen changes spacial relationships, the more so the closer the camera approaches a subject. In the Cinemascope format, where the screen is more than twice as wide as its height, there is space for two close-ups in the one frame; and the medium shot still allows more of the surroundings to be seen than many long shots in the standard format do. Thus widescreen movies allow the film maker to show the particular individual in close detail either along with one or two other individuals, or against his background. Thus, it can be seen that this format makes possible a new kind of filmic relationship between the character and his environment.

PLATES 31, 32 AND 33. Normal, high and low angles. Not only do high and low angles give one character dominance over the other, they also raise (high angle) and lower (low angle) the horizon.

PLATE 33. (See caption opposite).

High and low angles

The camera does not have to be at the same level as its subject, but can be either higher or lower. There exists a filmic convention that a high angle shot of a character (that is one in which the camera looks down at him) makes the viewer feel more powerful than him. Conversely a low angle shot places the character apparently above the viewer, and can impress him with his power. This system can be extended so that one character is shown (by low angle camera) as stronger than another (seen from a high angle). This commonplace convention derives from certain kinds of social behaviour. The tactic, for example, of the boss who places his employee in a low chair and stands up to lecture him is well known.

However, high and low angles can be used in ways totally divorced from this kind of naturalistic connection. Indeed they can be achieved from positions so dizzyingly far from our daily experience that we cannot but note their strangeness. Orson Welles directed his camera to shoot the contents of a room apparently from the ceiling; on another occasion he placed his camera almost under the foot of a monstrous figure as he steps from his car. Examples of this kind show us something new: that the camera, wherever it is placed, creates for its viewer a point of view. This may be naturalistic or it may be altogether fantastic.

Point of view

The camera may be thought of as an agent – a kind of go-between – that looks upon the scene on our behalf. Doing so it takes up and positions us in a certain point of view. The idea is not quite as simple as it seems, for that point of view will seldom resemble that which a human witness to a scene might expect to obtain.

Subjective point of view

Occasionally, usually for no more than part of a scene, the camera may indeed take up the position of a character, either looking on the action from the point at which he looks, or seeing it over his shoulder. These are two variants of a device called 'subjective point of view': the audience actually takes up for a while the point of view of the character. Alternatively the camera may scrutinise the actions and reactions of one character so closely that the audience seems to begin to feel his responses to what goes on around him. This is a further variant of the subjective point of view.

Objective point of view

Subjective ways of seeing rarely last for more than a few moments, and the camera is more usually placed so that it takes up an objective role. As we have already mentioned, functioning in this mode it does not provide an obvious equivalent for the eye of the human observer. None the less, it is possible to speak of it establishing a point of view. How should this be understood?

A useful way to see how 'objective point of view' works is to examine one of its predominant patterns, known as 'privileged point of view'. The idea of privileging a point of view is to give the spectator more information of a certain kind about the scene in front of him than he could possibly have got had he witnessed it in life. The camera moves from place to place, from shot to shot, to show him all he needs to know to satisfy the questions the film's story raises at that moment. So the camera placings required to create a privileged point of view have to be chosen in co-ordination with the events passing in the screenplay to give the viewer a particular insight into them. This model explains the organisation of the vast bulk of commercially made feature films and television series, so it can readily be seen in operation. The total effect is comparable to that achieved in the novel by the omniscient narrator, the voice that tells the story, knowing and revealing everything the author decides the reader needs to know.

Let us assume that A walks up to B, speaks to him briefly, then knocks him to the ground with a punch. This action could be covered in extreme

PLATE 34. Objective point of view of two girls.

PLATE 35. Subjective shot taken from the point of view of one girl.

long shot which would give us objective, but not privileged coverage. A privileged point of view would give the spectator the answer to various questions the action might raise in his mind. In this instance he would want to discover what was on the mind of A, and a shot taken closer to the two characters, perhaps looking at A from over the shoulder of B, would satisfy this desire. But then the viewer would want to know how B reacts to the things A has to say, and the shot we have just set up would not show him; so the action would now be cut to a third shot, possibly the counterpart of the second, but now looking at B from over the shoulder of A.

This kind of pattern can be much extended, and we shall look at a fuller example when we examine the style of cutting that complements this method of shooting (page 115). There could, of course, be many other ways of covering this scene and giving the spectator a privileged point of view. It is conceivable (if grotesque) to think that it could have been done through giant extreme close-ups of the lips of the two angry men. But this is not the point. What we need to notice is that a simple scene has been fragmented into shots which put the viewer into a special, privileged position. This is turn enables him to pick up certain pieces of visible information which the action motivates him to want to see. The notion of privileged point of view thus embraces a whole way of constructing film narrative; it does not describe one particular way of shooting a scene (as the notion of shooting exclusively through extreme close-ups suggests). There are many different ways of presenting privileged points of view for any one scene.

Thus the point of view of the camera puts the viewer into a certain relation with the action. That this relation will be different in the subjective and the objective positions is easily understood. That objective points of view differ from one another can be recognised when we return to compare the kind of privileged point of view we imagined for our little violent scene with the static objectivity of a single establishing shot through which the entire action might be filmed. These differences in point of view will radically affect both what the spectator sees, and thus what he knows; and, according to his closeness to certain fragments of the action, the way that he responds emotionally to what he sees.

Lenses

Once again we have been relying on certain unspoken assumptions: acknowledging that the camera can be moved from point to point, we have none the less assumed that it sees with an eye that reduplicates human vision. We must now revise our approach, because in fact the human eye and the camera lens function in quite different ways.

The eye selects in a way that the lens cannot. Imagine yourself sitting in a room and taking tea with a friend. As you eat you talk, and the conversation grows more and more interesting; but suddenly you notice your friend has let a large crumb fall into his beard, and you find you cannot take your eyes off it. In this little example we must assume that you do not move from your seat, and that without moving your head or your eyes you can take in about half the room by using your full field of vision. Yet from that same position when a mere crumb catches your attention, your mind will concentrate on that tiny area of your field of vision, examining it in detail, and ignoring all that lies around it. The rest of the field is still visible, but you pay it no heed, so in a certain sense it is also invisible. This capability for selective viewing arises from the direction of the eyes by the mind, the mind scrutinising only that part of the image that takes its attention.

The camera does not work in the same way when it is equipped with lenses of 'fixed focal length'. And although the 'zoom lens' can mimic that effect, it does so imperfectly, and is a special case that will be dealt with last. Lenses of fixed focal length simply transmit to the emulsion all that comes within their field of vision. That is one reason why the camera must be positioned with care. But there are different kinds of fixed focal length lenses, and each has its defining characteristics that alter the picture it produces.

Lenses of fixed focal length

From our point of view as analysts of the image, it is enough if we know that lenses of fixed focal length have an unchanging 'angle of acceptance' (that is width of view), and constant 'depth of field' characteristics (see page 65). Broadly speaking there are three classes of such lenses.

Standard lenses

These most nearly duplicate the vision of the human eye in that they provide a roughly comparable width of view (or angle of acceptance); and the image they render has a scale of perspective much the same as that of the eye. Perspective may be described as the effect caused by the apparent shrinking of objects the further they are from the spectator. With the standard lens, objects have roughly the same proportion in relation to their distance as would be expected in life, and this gives the image created by the standard lens a seeming perspective comparable to that which we experience with our own eyes. Thus our sense of distance within the picture corresponds with the sense of distance we would expect to obtain if we saw the scene with our own eyes. Perspective matters a great deal to the cinematographer because it is one of the means by which he can create a sense of the third dimension, of depth in a two dimensional image.

PLATE 36. Landscape shot taken with a standard lens.

PLATE 37. Landscape shot taken with a wide angle lens from the same position as Plate 36.

PLATE 38. Landscape shot taken with a telephoto lens from the same position as Plates 36 and 37.

Wide angle lenses

As their name implies these lenses have a wider angle of acceptance than the human eye, and take in a broader view than the eye does in a single glance. This produces exciting consequences. An interesting distortion is caused when that wider angle of view is reproduced on the screen, for the screen of course does not change in size whatever lens is mounted on the camera: there is in effect a slight compression of the image, which affects the perception of perspective. The wide angle lens appears to deepen perspective, making objects shrink more rapidly in proportion to their distance than they do before the naked eye.

If the camera looks over the shoulder of one character at another, the distance between them in depth is measured by our judging their relative sizes. The wide angle lens makes the nearer character look larger than he would to the eye, and the farther character appears smaller. But when the eye sees this distorted image displayed on the screen it reconstructs perspective according to the scale it knows from its daily experience. As a consequence it interprets the picture rendered by the wide angle lens as showing a greater depth than it does; in our example the viewer sees the two characters as further apart than they actually were. The wide angle lens increases apparent depth.

There are a number of ways in which the distortions of this lens can be productively employed – and with the wider lenses such distortions can be severe. The wide angle of acceptance makes the lens handy for filming in smaller locations. A standard lens will take only a fragment of a small room, where the wide lens might cover most of it. Sometimes this principle can be exploited in reverse so that movie sets can be constructed to smaller dimensions (which saves expense) than they are to appear to have on screen. The wide lens restores their supposed dimensions.

Creative uses of the wide angle lens often exploit its distortion of depth. If, for example, a screenplay concerns characters who are hostile to each other, their emotional distance can readily be expressed in visual terms by the wide lens. The director uses it to keep the characters apart visually, and the distance they have between them on the screen comes to signify the emotional gap between them. Countless films have made this metaphor into a convention, the most famous of them being Orson Welles's *Citizen Kane* (1941).

The increase in apparent depth which this lens creates alters the perception of the speed of people or objects moving between the camera and the horizon. A camera equipped with a standard lens and set to look down a mile of railroad track will represent this track as a mile long; and a train moving towards the camera will seem to be travelling at its true speed – let us say 60 mph. Now imagine the same scene shot through a wide angle lens that makes the track appear to be two miles long. Although the train actually travels the same distance in the same time (and therefore at the same speed), the distance *looks* twice as great, and the train consequently *appears* to be going at twice the speed. This distortion is much loved by film makers who want to increase perceived speed. It can be equally dramatic indoors, where for instance a character apparently at a considerable distance across the room can approach another in the foreground at unexpected speed simply by walking towards him.

Telephoto lenses

It is not difficult to foresee at this point that the distortions of the telephoto lens are the converse of the wide angle lens. A telephoto, or long focal lens has a narrower angle of acceptance than the human eye, and the very long lenses have a very narrow angle of acceptance indeed. Inevitably certain distortions to the image result when it is reproduced on the unvarying screen. A degree of stretching may be noticed in the image, but, most obvious, it will seem to have been foreshortened. It is a primary characteristic of the telephoto lens that it appears to flatten perspective, making objects diminish in proportion less rapidly as they move into the distance than they appear to do to the eye. In portrait or close-up work this effect makes the face look fatter than in actuality.

The telephoto lens has familiar uses that almost speak for themselves.

They are ideal for obtaining close-up pictures of people and objects that are far away, and are employed by animal watchers and sports cinematographers and newsmen for that reason. Indeed those uses have encouraged the development of a convention in thrillers where a familiar function of the telephoto lens is to cover a character who is seen in close-up from far off. This device transmits effectively to the viewer the feeling that he is spying on the character. As that example suggests, while the wide lens tends to include not only the character, but a great deal that surrounds him, the telephoto lens excludes, often not merely the surroundings, but perhaps everything other than head and shoulders. It is a highly selective lens.

It also affects the perceived speed of objects travelling towards the camera. The railroad track that we imagined a moment ago now appears shorter than in actuality, the mile seeming no more than perhaps half that distance. The train, still travelling at the same pace, appears to move only at half the speed. Thus simply by changing lenses we have pushed our train up to 120 mph, and now slowed it to some 30 mph. This is a useful way of demonstrating just how effectively the cinema can distort actuality.

Focus

Lenses have another important variable in their capacity to focus selectively. This means that in most circumstances the film maker chooses at what range to set his focus so that some objects within the frame are seen to be sharp, and others are blurred. This matters to the viewer because it is easier to get information from what we can see clearly than from what we have to puzzle over to recognise. So we tend to look first at what is sharp, then at the parts that are out of focus. Knowing this, a director can shape our attention, having us look, for instance, at a character sharply focussed who stands against a blurred background, which for that reason does not distract our attention. Or with two characters in frame, a film maker can direct our eyes at one by having him in, and the other man out of focus. If he wishes to switch our attention as the scene progresses, he can 'pull focus' so that the first person goes out of focus and the second comes into sharp vision. Thus by observing the way a shot is focussed we get yet another indication of how the film makers meant to direct our eyes.

Depth of field

When a lens is focussed on an object it will often be noticed that more than the object itself is acceptably sharp. To illustrate we will return to the railroad track. If the camera is pointed down the track and focussed

PLATES 39 AND 40. Focus selects areas of the image for our attention. Pulling focus switches attention elsewhere.

on a long shot of, let us say, a signal light, we will notice firstly that anything at equal distance from the camera (that is on the 'focal plane') is equally sharply focussed. But if we look at the sleepers, we will observe that a number of them in front of and also beyond the signal will look sharp before we come to the point where focus falls detectably away. This area of acceptable focus before and behind the precise focal plane is known as the 'depth of field' of the image. The extent of that depth of field itself varies according to a number of factors.

Distance

The closer to the lens the focal plane is set, the less the depth of field. While in our example the signal, in long shot, stood in a moderately deep field of focus, a close-up of a child taken with the same lens might have a depth of field so shallow that the nose and ears of the face could not be kept in focus simultaneously.

Lens efficiency

The more light that falls on a subject, the tighter the aperture of the iris in the lens through which it passes to modulate the exposure. This is a technical matter, and it is enough for us to recognise that the more light a crew can bring to bear on the subject, the more efficiently its lenses can be allowed to work, and therefore the greater the depth of field. It follows directly that deep focus interior work can be expensive because it requires that extra illumination to get the best out of the lenses.

Focal length of the lens

The most obvious factor in the control of depth of field, in so far as the spectator will notice it, is the type of lens selected. The wide angle lens reproduces by far the deepest field of focus, the telephoto lens the shallowest, and these features are so marked that no film maker would choose one of these lenses without considering this factor.

The very deep field of focus obtainable with the wide angle lens makes it practicable in many circumstances to have everything within the picture frame, from an object very close to the camera through to the horizon, in focus. It will be recalled that we can look readily at everything in focus, so it becomes apparent that if a director arranges his picture with care, the audience will relate all the parts of it. To return to the railroad track, we now have very close to us a baby sitting on the line, in the middle distance a signal set at go, and in the far distance a train approaching. Shot with a wide lens, everything is in focus, the audience relates all that it sees, and gets a nasty impression (worsened by the accelerated speed of the train that the lens produces) that an ugly accident is about to occur. The shallow field of focus of the telephoto lens leaves out of focus everything that is not either on or very close to the focal plane. Back at the railroad we would find that a long shot with a really long focal lens might show of the scene described above nothing

PLATE 41. Shallow depth of field.

PLATE 42. Deep field of focus. In this shot, while the focal plane is still set on the stone seat, acceptably sharp focus extends a long way down the lane.

but the front of the train. If the signal should happen to be in frame, it would remain completely out of focus, and if the baby should stray into the shot it would be so totally blurred that it would be unrecognisable as no more than a soft 'bloom' on the image. Such a shot would of course slow down the speed of the train, but it could be effective as a means of suggesting its enormous weight, and its inevitable, relentless progress.

Characteristics of fixed focal length lenses: summary

The wide angle lens
This lens relates characters or objects by keeping them sharply in focus even while it separates them in depth, and shows them set in their surroundings. It can be recognised by the deep perspective it creates, and by the way it exaggerates speed. The director employing such a lens has the opportunity to stretch space and shrink time, and he may well use this feature expressively.

The telephoto lens
This lens flattens perspectives, slows up true speed, selects actors or objects from out of their surroundings, and seems to enlarge them. It creates a shallow depth of field. In contrast to the wide angle lens, it gives the illusion of shrinking space and stretching time.

The standard lens
This lens has properties which fall between those of the wide angle and the telephoto lenses. It will be recognised as in service when perspectives and speeds appear roughly as the eye expects them in the real world. It can create a relatively broad, but not infinite depth of field.

The zoom lens

Since the late 1950s the zoom lens has become efficient and popular. Its more formal name, the 'variable focal length lens', reveals its function in that, unlike the fixed lenses, the zoom lens can be adjusted by movement of a simple lever or a power drive (the 'zoom') so that it shifts from one focal length to another. As it does so, it shifts from one angle of acceptance to another by a smooth transition. This can be done while the camera is running, so that a shot that begins on a wide angle can conclude with the lens having been zoomed forward to a telephoto setting. This has the effect of progressively excluding much of the original image and of enlarging the part the shot ends on. There are many further uses for the zoom lens, the main ones being the following:

Substitution for fixed lenses
Sometimes the zoom is not operated at all as a shot is taken, but the lens will still be used to advantage. In this case the cameraman operates the

zoom before the shot is taken in order to set the frame to precisely the focal length he requires, whether on a wide, standard, or telephoto setting. During any take the image looks as if it were shot through a fixed lens. There are minor technical differences, but the layman will not detect them. Brought into service in this way, the zoom lens is a convenience that speeds work and its convenience may encourage the more adventurous film maker to use a variety of different lens lengths for successive shots. In turn this has permitted a more imaginative use of the camera, a change which, as we shall see, came with other developments that made possible more rapid movement, and a swifter response to action by the camera.

Reframing a moving subject

In this case the zoom is operated as the camera runs as a means of keeping a moving subject at a constant size in the frame. This commonplace device keeps the viewer in an unchanging relation with the subject, whether near or far. Thus a sense of intimacy with a character may develop if the frame keeps him in close shot as he walks along and conversely a sense of estrangement may arise if the moving frame keeps a character perpetually in long shot. This is a specialised version of the best known use of the zoom.

The false tracking shot

In this instance the zoom lens is operated vigorously in a shot which at first glance makes it seem that the camera is either approaching or moving away from the subject. Amateur cinematographers, until they know better, love this punch-in-the-eye effect; it is, however, tedious to watch when overused.

In fact the zoom does not affect the image in the way the camera moving on a dolly does. As it moves towards the longer focal lengths, the zoom simply enlarges a section of the image, so it actually seems that the subject is approaching the camera rather than the camera drawing nearer to the subject. This can be disconcerting. If a cameraman zooms forward on, say, a horseman riding over a mountain range, not only the horse and rider, but also the whole landscape, appear to hurl themselves towards the viewer. Usually camera operators try to disguise this disruptive effect. One solution of the problem is to have a character move across the frame, and to zoom forward or backwards as he goes; in this instance the movement of the character helps to disguise the movement of the zoom.

Conveying information through the zoom

Though the moving camera alters images in a different way from the zoom, the two methods of camera movement can both serve to add new information to a shot in similar ways:

(1) *Revealing fresh information.* When the camera or zoom lens is pulled back from the original subject, it reveals what had previously been concealed. Typically a shot may start in close-up on a character and pull back to reveal where he is, or to whom he is speaking. Such a device may be used, for example, to surprise the audience at the start of a sequence.

(2) *Examination of detail.* When, conversely, after a start on a wide shot, the camera or lens is moved forward, it can close in on the subject. The closer shot makes it possible for the audience to see details that were not visible before.

Movement

We need to consider both what happens when the subject moves, and what happens when the camera makes one of the many kinds of movement of which it is capable.

Movement of the subject

The cinema is an art of movement, and the importance of movement to the art is demonstrated by the way the viewer's eye responds to it. In Part 2 we noted that the eye will tend to be attracted to a bright area rather than to a dark area; if one part of the image is in focus and another is blurred, the eye looks at the sharp area; and again it gives priority to areas in the frame that are richly coloured as opposed to those that are drab. At this point we have to remark that movement has an overriding impact on the eye. Whatever else happens in the picture, movement before all else catches the attention of the viewer.

This is a basic element in human response, possibly because mankind discovered early that whatever moves may be dangerous. Whatever its origins, the actor cannot overlook it. If he moves while another performer is still, the audience will tend to switch its attention to him. So actors tend to co-ordinate their movements with the moment-by-moment requirements of their roles. If, for example, another character is speaking, and the audience should be looking at him, the listening actor will not make a sharp movement until it falls to him to draw the eyes of the spectators. The cinema has borrowed this essential control of movement from the stage.

Movement on the screen can be dramatised more effectively than that on the stage because the camera controls and shifts the point of view. Every member of the audience in live theatre has no other view of the action but that from the position of his seat; he cannot, furthermore, inspect details of the character or action in close-up as a cinema audience might. But despite these relative limitations, actors on the stage do move about in such a way as to increase or decrease the authority of their presence at given moments. Comparable movements can be arranged on the screen. If an actor moves towards the camera, the volume of space his image takes in the frame increases. He actually grows bigger to the eye, and as he does so he takes up a more important position in the frame, tending increasingly to dominate the action. The converse happens when he moves away. This is not to say that an actor in long shot cannot dominate another in close-up, but if he is to do so something more than his position in the frame (perhaps his role, or what he is saying) will be required to give him that greater authority.

Movement of the camera

The camera can either be moved on its own axes (that is it can be turned while standing on the same spot), or it can be moved bodily.

Axial movement

Turning on its axis the camera is said to 'pan' (the word comes from panorama). The commonest such movement is the *horizontal pan*, of which two types can be distinguished which provide the observer with further clues to the film makers' intentions. The 'survey pan' simply reveals all there is to see beyond the limits of the frame. Thus to show the contents of a room, or a landscape, the camera performs a survey pan. Ordinarily this will be an objective use of the camera.

Alternatively the camera may follow a moving subject, and then it is said to perform a 'tracking pan'. If the subject is a person, the tracking pan can serve to build identification, and thus subjectivity, because the individual observed is held steady in the frame as he moves. Meanwhile everything about him shifts and passes out of frame, remaining visible for a shorter time than the character.

The camera can also move in a *vertical pan*, which in the nature of things will more often survey than follow.

Shots taken when the camera moves bodily from point to point tend to have greater visual impact. The several names of travelling shots derive from the various means by which the camera is carried, each of which makes possible different kinds of shot.

Dolly, tracking, and trucking shots

These are all similar in that the camera is mounted on a wheeled vehicle, for movement across a flat-floored room in the case of a dolly; on rails across sets or locations when it tracks; and usually on a powered vehicle (often an adapted truck) in the last case. The dolly is slowest of these transports, the truck potentially the fastest. All are capable of imparting a smooth glide to camera movement.

Crane and helicopter shots

Such shots free the camera from the earth's surface. Cranes are now manufactured to remarkable sophistication. For studio work they may be purpose built on a relatively small scale; for location work they can be made to huge sizes. There are also precisely guided cranes oriented by computer for shooting models and miniatures. The helicopter shot (precisely what its name suggests) of course gives the film maker a very different range of possibilities, but also a new set of technical problems which can be easily imagined.

Like tracking vehicles, cranes and helicopters move the camera smoothly, and communicate a vivid sense of pleasure to the viewer who experiences all the power of movement without having to put any effort into it. The dreamlike movement of this gliding, effortless quality becomes all the more magical when the camera draws the viewer into the air and gives him flight.

Though we have treated axial and bodily movements of the camera as separate entities, they frequently combine to create a *compound movement*. So the camera might pan while tracking forward and rising on the arm of a crane, for instance. Such a movement would demand the co-ordination of a larger crew of operators, and inevitably would cost more than a simple movement. But it can hardly be stressed too strongly that complex movement furnishes the cinema with one of its sweetest pleasures, fulfilling for the viewer desires for freedom of movement and vision which he is unlikely to be able to satisfy readily elsewhere.

The remaining two kinds of movement by their nature are compound.

Handheld shots

Again these shots are just what their name implies, though some operators prefer to mount the camera on the shoulder for greater stability. The viewer can identify this method of camera operation by looking for an unevenness of movement that can usually be detected at the edges of the frame.

Carrying the camera has the advantage for the operator that it frees him to react more immediately to what he sees than when he has to co-ordinate the crew of a dolly or a crane. Originally, therefore, handheld shots appealed to those who wanted to cover live action, and this remains the case to this day – for not only can the cameraman react swiftly to developments about him, but the typically uneven movement of the camera communicates the sense of a more lively, immediate relationship with the subject than the polished gliding of the studio camera suggests. Since documentary and news coverage on television have long since confirmed the association, feature film makers now find they can make use of it to give a similar sense of immediacy to their work. It has also become commonplace to employ the shaky movement of the handheld shot as a visual metaphor in scenes where the script calls for the communication of fear.

Steadicam
This recent innovation provides the cameraman with a device which enables him to move fast over uneven ground without the shocks of his movement transmitting themselves to the picture frame. The camera is mounted on a damped suspension which in turn fits onto the operator through a body harness. It gives the picture an eerie, floating movement, quite unlike anything in daily experience. Its unworldliness suited and enhanced the atmosphere of Stanley Kubrick's *The Shining* (1980).

Movement and point of view

It is worth reminding ourselves that the moving camera produces a different change to the image from a zoom lens. Not only does the camera appear to move towards the subject rather than the reverse, but it seems to move in three dimensional space. This effect arises because objects grow or shrink at a rate proportional to their distance from the lens. But in another respect the mobile camera and zoom lens have the same effect, that movement with a character tends to increase subjectivity, while movement in a contrary direction is likely to distance the viewer.

That camera movement in relation to the subject can, if the narrative runs that way, change the audience's feelings towards a character, emphasises the fact that as it moves the camera changes the audience's point of view. It is for this reason that camera movement can be such a subtle matter: when an editor cuts from one static camera position to another, the change in point of view is relatively abrupt. But a moving camera almost undetectably moves us to a new viewing point, and subtly changes our relation with the action on screen. Those changes are too various to fall into easily identified types. The student of the screen needs to be aware that they happen, and to watch for their effect. As an illustration, the camera might glide in from a distant point of view, and take up a relation of great intimacy with a character; it might stay close to him, or after a time move away to set him firmly back in the environment from which it had singled him out. There are unlimited possibilities.

Editing in camera

Camera movement has another aspect to it, namely that it can provide an alternative for the assembly of a number of different shots. Take the example just given. The moving camera conveys in just one shot what would otherwise have required a minimum of three shots to express. With a static camera it would have been necessary, at the very least, to start with an extreme long shot, to cut into a medium close-up, and to cut back to a long shot. Those shots would have been assembled on the editing table. With the moving camera they are brought together, and the effect is of a disguised change of shot. 'Editing in camera', as this stylistic device is called, makes for smooth transitions, and for a sense of uninterrupted time which the assembled scene would not have. The sense of flowing time is particularly significant: it is often described as being more realistic since time in actual life does not suffer the kind of fragmentation it can undergo on the editing bench.

Movement and time

Time changes in the cinema. It goes without saying that it must do since the audience could not, for instance, sit around for seventy years to watch *The Life and Times of Judge Roy Bean* (John Huston, 1972). We shall investigate how film leaves out great chunks of life when we deal with editing; but there are other ways in which films subtly bend time. One of these is by movement of the camera.

When we go to the cinema, we find nothing of great interest to look at but the screen, and when the lights go down and the colours and sounds spill from the screen, a good movie captures the whole of our attention. (Incidentally, this is one of the ways in which cinema differs from television, which has to compete with the many other things that go on in the typical home.) What happens to our sense of time when our attention is seized? It is convenient to separate out two aspects of our daily experience of time. The first is our rational knowledge. We know – because our watches, clocks and radios tell us so – that time passes in an even, measured way, twenty four hours a day, eight of them at work, eight asleep, and so on. However, we *experience* time according to the degree our attention is captured. As students we know that we have spent an hour at a certain lecture because our watches tell us so. But that lecture could seem to last two hours or more if it is dull and uninformative. On the other hand a lively and interesting teacher could have made the same period seem to pass in a matter of minutes.

Film deals with time as we experience it, and it alters that experience in a whole lot of often unnoticed ways. Any film sets up a rhythm of its own as can be appreciated when we think of the difference between the rhythm of a suspenseful police thriller and that of a love story or a musical. Those rhythms derive in part from the events of the story; thus every film has its own rhythm. But rhythm also arises from the way we give our attention: what happens on the screen will take us time to digest, and the more unexpected or complicated the event, the longer our reaction time. The passage of that reaction time affects our experience of time. Thus every event in film – and not just every event in the plot – affects the audience's perception of time.

Among the events that change our experience of the screen is movement. Movement is rhythmic event within the film. It affects the tempo or rhythm of a shot because it is an event that changes the relationships between all three of the characters, their background and the audience. Since, as we have said, the audience's sensing of a film's tempo gives it the measure of the passing of filmic time, camera movement will affect perception of the rate of time passing. Again it has to be stressed there are an unlimited number of permutations, and it is not possible to say that specific movements affect the audience's perceptions in specific ways. The general truth of the assertion can, however, be checked by imagining a simple example. A man walks along a lonely road. We track up to him. In the first instance we track fast, perhaps approaching at the speed of a car; in the second we come up to him slowly, barely at walking pace. These two shots of the same subject will not only feel different, they will give the viewer a quite different sense of time, as they cover the same distance at different speeds.

The use of distortion

Distortions of time

The camera itself can distort time by means other than tracking. Since movie projectors run at a constant speed of twenty-four frames per second, the camera has to do the same if time is to pass at the same speed on screen. If the camera is run fast, the reduction of speed when the film passes through the projector at its unvarying twenty-four frames per second causes 'slow motion' on the screen. Conversely, 'accelerated motion' results from running the camera slower than normal.

Slow motion
There are several possible consequences of reducing speed:

(1) It can make a very fast action visible: a bullet is seen as it shatters a target. This application is often exploited in scientific films.
(2) It may make a familiar action unreal: the bodyweight seems to increase and, according to narrative context, this may either make an actor's movement seem laborious and unending, or graceful and serene. The latter application was more popular for some years after the success of Bo Widerberg's *Elvira Madigan* (1967) in which the heroine runs joyously through meadows with long hair spilling behind her. Hardly a shampoo commercial has since been made without a predictable swirl of slow motion hair past the lens.

(3) It emphasises moments of great dramatic excitement – a crash, a fight, something critical of that kind. This use seems to have developed as a filmic metaphor for the way people often describe seeing things happen at moments of crisis as if they were in slow motion. A modern variant of this stylistic device is 'stopped motion' in which every second or third frame is printed twice, which produces a jerky and slow motion.

Accelerated motion (or undercranking)
This device can have the following effects:

(1) It can make a very slow action visible: a flower unfurls, flourishes and dies. This function again finds its main use in scientific films.
(2) It can render a familiar action absurd. Bodyweight appears to reduce if motion is sufficiently accelerated, and human movements become jerky and ridiculous. It is an old comic device.
(3) In certain applications it increases the appearance of power. To this day car chases on screen are usually shown in accelerated motion, and are more thrilling for doing so.

Freeze frame
A final distortion of motion is to stop it altogether, which is done by reprinting the same frame indefinitely. It can have the momentary effect of reducing the film to the status of a photograph.

Distortions of the image

Filters
The presence of distorting lenses is easily enough noticed not to need comment, but filters are seldom detected by the untrained eye, and they have a critical role in enhancing the image. It is a function that complements that of the lighting. The filter itself is a piece of glass that is placed in front of the lens and all light that enters the camera passes through it. According to the property of the glass, the image may, as a result, have one colour or another enhanced – the sky may be darkened and the clouds picked out; complexions may change tone or freckles seem to stand out more. As in day-for-night shooting (see page 43) the effect may be to make a scene marvellously unreal.

Gels
Gel is sometimes smeared on the whole or part of a lens to soften the edges of the subject. It was very fashionable in Hollywood in the 1930s, specially in films dealing with the emotional lives of women. The softening of the image stood as a visual metaphor for romance.

Gauzes
These were most extensively employed at about the same period and in the same kind of woman's film. Their visual effect is comparable, but

PLATES 43 AND 44. Two shots taken within a few seconds, Plate 43 with no filter, and Plate 44 with a red filter. By stopping the blue light this filter darkens the sky and distinguishes it from the clouds.

they can lead to a more complete blurring of the image. Often placed selectively over only part of the lens, the gauze would blend the human figure, which might be seen in some clarity, into a background which might blend indefinably into the surrounding light.

Composition in the frame

By this point in our description of the many variables the cameraman controls, it ought to be apparent that the picture can be organised with considerable care. The composition of a picture means the way that it has been organised to guide the eyes of spectators and to lead them to certain areas before others. In turn this implies that parts of a picture may yield meaning before others.

What happens without such organisation can be experienced by anyone who has the chance to see examples of early cinema – films made during the first ten years of the industry from 1895. Typically in such pieces a number of characters perform by moving along an imaginary line that runs from one side of the frame to the other. They do not move in depth, and no attempt is made to create an impression of the third dimension. The characters are not singled out from each other, as the convention of the close-up had not yet evolved. Often several characters will act at once, gesticulating wildly at each other, and very likely running back and forth. The viewer does not know at which to look as the movement is so general it draws his eyes from place to place in the picture without showing him what to understand, nor even who is the most important figure in the action at any moment. For these reasons early films can be exhausting to watch. The almost complete lack of composition in so many of them tells us how much this aspect of film making helps guide the audience's attention in the more sophisticated productions to which we are accustomed.

As with all the aspects of visual style with which we are dealing, there are no fixed rules according to which picture composition must be arranged. None the less, conventions do exist. Some, like the use of perspective to give a sense of depth, have had long life (in that case, since the Renaissance). Others, such as Antonioni's placing of blank walls in a position in frame where they block perspective and render his images relatively two-dimensional, may be associated with the work of one director only.

The frame

The importance of the frame for the viewer is that it provides him with the only means he has to take his bearings on the action. That may seem an absurd thing to say since the frame is always there, as the screen, in front of the audience; but its very permanence emphasises its significance. It is the only constant in cinema. All composition is organised in relation to the frame. Let us take a simple example.

Imagine a medium close shot of a person who is looking at someone else. His eyes look out to a point beyond and to the right of the camera. If this character is framed so that his image falls to the left of the picture, he looks towards – and is balanced by – an area or mass of space of roughly equal volume to the right. In pictorial conventions familiar to the West, this would be a well balanced image. However if the same character in the same attitude should be framed to the right of the picture, he would have a large area of space empty behind his head, and would be looking towards a frame line that would be uncomfortably close to his eyes on the right. According to the same conventions, this would make for an unbalanced, rather claustrophobic image; and a director would call for it only if he wished to add to a feeling of discomfort about this character. The difference is accounted for simply by the placing of the actor within the frame.

Organisation of visual information

The example above gives an indication that *mass* has to be considered as an element of pictorial composition. If most of the frame is occupied by a vast building which towers over an individual who takes up only a fragment of screen space, the disposition of mass within the picture frame makes a visual point – perhaps about the oppressed nature of that man's life. Mass and proportion, then, have intimate links. A character who dominates the foreground (and occupies the greater space) will tend visibly to dominate another character who is squeezed into what remains of the frame in the background. The film maker may choose to work with proportion as an expressive device. Our example above would be one way of doing this; but we have encountered many ways in which lenses can distort images, and as they do so they can alter the relative proportion of the objects within the frame.

The main means of composing the picture have already been described in our survey of the way the camera and lighting crews can control the attention of the viewer. Light and dark; sharp and soft focus; brilliant colour and the lack of it; movement and rest – all can be directed to organising not only the picture but the way the viewer reacts to it.

Two major factors with which we have not dealt also control the audience's attention. The first is, of course, the narrative. If a story is following one character, we will tend to follow him from shot to shot unless something, or some other character intrudes upon our attention. For the way we react to a shot depends on both what we have already seen, and what we expect will happen next. Thus the same shot would mean something different to us if it were placed in two very different parts of a film (because of what the audience has experienced during the film, shots of a tranquil sea would have a different significance at the beginning and end of Stephen Spielberg's *Jaws* (1975), for instance).

In Bo Widerberg's superb nineteenth-century romantic melodrama, *Elvira Madigan* (1967) mentioned above, the heroine, seen bathed in backlighting, in slow motion, and to an exquisite *adagio* by Mozart, runs across a summery meadow. The camera pans and swirls with her, and as it does so it pans across an entire film crew. They are on screen for fully a quarter of a second, a relatively long period in the context of the speed of human perception. Yet no one ever seems to notice this extraordinary spectacle, though it is there in plain view for anyone who should happen to be looking for it. In fact Widerberg's images at this point conform so completely to the narrative purpose (they illustrate the total commitment of the girl to her love affair) that the viewer cannot perceive the small mistake that has been made. The camera crew is effectively invisible.

A second factor in the composition of the picture has inescapable ties with narrative. As it is part of the work of the film crew to control it, it requires detailed consideration. It is of course the building of the soundtrack.

Part 4

Sound

The microphone and the ear

In one crucial way the microphone and the camera can be compared. Each picks up and relays for recording all the signals that come within its range. In the case of the camera we saw that it will photograph whatever falls within the angle of acceptance of its lenses. Broadly speaking the equivalent holds true for the microphone and tape recorder – that they will record whatever sounds fall within their range. In other words sound recording systems are not inherently any more selective than cameras: selection is left to the operator.

Contrast the performance of the equipment with that of human intelligence. We discovered earlier that the eye and mind work together to make a constant selection from, and mental enlargement of the visual information they receive. Something similar can be said of the work of the ear and the mind. This can be easily checked. When we are concentrating on reading, we do not experience much awareness of the sounds around us unless they are so loud they make it hard to think. But if we stop reading now for a moment, and listen, we become aware of layers of sound nearby, a little way off, and in the far distance, most of which our minds had cut out from consciously acknowledging as we were reading. It is possible to try the same test when talking to someone by switching attention away from the conversation for a moment and making oneself aware of the sounds that one has been ignoring. Other voices, radios, traffic, the wind, are often the unheard background to our lives.

Hearing, then, is selective. But the microphone, in broad terms is not. It follows that the soundtrack of a film is likely to have been constructed as carefully as the pictures to exclude at least some of the sound which might otherwise be present if all the sound that could be heard as the shots were taken were to be relayed without further change to the audience. In fact the building of soundtracks usually follows one of two approaches to dialogue and sound effects. Either the crew prepares, on behalf of the listener, something near a complete preselection of sound. The listener hears a track virtually all of which relates directly to the context of the film, the processes of mental digestion, so to speak, having been carried out for him by the sound crew. Alternatively the listener hears a track which is charged with some elements that have no direct bearing on the narrative, where less preselection has taken place, and where he has to undertake an interpretation of the information for himself. We shall return to this stylistic difference later.

There is one vital difference between the way the ear and the eye operate. The eye finds great difficulty in looking at more than one thing at a time. It can look at one thing *and then* another, and back and forwards between them with great rapidity – an ability on which the editing process relies. When the screen is divided into two areas (for example, on television a darts player throws his dart in one segment of the screen and it hits the board in the other), and the action follows a predictable order, the eye copes by looking first at one segment, then at the other. But where (as in the title sequences of *The Thomas Crown Affair* (1968) and *The Boston Strangler* (1968) the screen divides into many segments, all simultaneously throwing up new information, the eye cannot cope, and the spectator experiences a degree of tension. That, it goes without saying, is what the makers of these thrillers wanted to inflict on their audiences from the start of their movies, but it makes the point that in such circumstances the eye has been asked to do more than it is capable of doing.

By contrast, the ear quite readily digests information from more than one source simultaneously, provided those sources do not require detailed interpretation. Most people cannot attend to more than one conversation at a time, but can listen to a conversation, various sound effects, and perhaps music. This capability matters to the film maker because it enables him to interweave such elements in his soundtrack as he takes it through the several stages of recording, selection and mixing.

Sound equipment

Microphones

Not all microphones are identical. The main difference we need to notice centres on their responsiveness to sound coming from a variety of directions.

Like a lens, a microphone (or 'mike') has an angle of acceptance, though it is by no means as specific as that of the lens. In fact what might be called the general service microphone has an omni-directional response – it picks up sounds from all round. Others are directional, and respond only to sounds originating in front of or behind the microphones – these are called figure-of-eight microphones. A further variant, known either as the cardioid or uni-directional microphone, picks up sound from in front only. A development of the last type has the microphone mounted in a long tube: this is the 'rifle mike', which has a very narrow angle of response, so that it can be 'aimed' at a speaker and will exclude much of the sound from around him.

In recent years a further method of recording the individual has been developed. This is the radio microphone, which an actor wears concealed in his costume and which picks up very little else besides his voice sound. This device incorporates a transmitter which broadcasts the signal to the tape recorder, and thus the performer is free to move without the restriction of cables or support booms.

While a television news crew may work with only a single rifle microphone so that they can record an interview in noisy surroundings, the range of microphones available enables the crew of a sophisticated production to preselect certain fields of sound when shooting live sound. In these circumstances a number of microphones will be deployed. There may be a radio mike on each of two or three main characters to record their dialogue; the sound recordists will then decide what further sound effects they want, and will place microphones accordingly – a technician may aim a rifle mike at the characters' feet, while an omni-directional mike could be placed at some distance to pick up some of the noises of the location, whether bird song or traffic rumble.

Thus the choice of microphones and their placing allow the sound crew to select to some extent the sounds they wish to record at the expense of others.

The mixer

The signals produced by a number of microphones set up on location after this fashion can be passed through a mixer before they reach the tape recorder. At this point the 'level' (or loudness) of each microphone's signal can be adjusted, and this gives the sound crew a further opportunity to 'arrange' sound by balancing one source against another. In most situations they are likely to decide to give priority to the voices of the actors; and such effects as are being picked up will therefore be mixed through at a lower level. But if for some reason the crew wanted to achieve a different effect, the sound of the environment could be mixed with the voices so that it dominated them.

The tape recorder

Although it seems too obvious to be worth remarking that the signals from the microphones are recorded on a tape recorder, this was not the case until the 1950s. The development of magnetic recorders gave film makers new freedoms with sound, its principal importance to them, apart from the high quality of reproduction, being the fact that they could now record the sound on a tape which could be edited as a separate entity. This factor makes it possible for the director at a later stage in production to decide whether to use the sound as he recorded it, whether to start the sound before cutting in the pictures, or vice versa, and whether to modulate (or alter) its quality. He can run the sound against other images, or can run the images without sound. He gains a freedom in the assembly of his finished picture which, as we shall come to understand, is very considerable.

The dubbing suite

So far we have assumed that the crew records sounds made as the picture is being shot. This is by no means always so; and even where it is, additional sound will often be added at a later stage. The 'dubbing suite', which is in effect a sophisticated sound recording studio in which the picture can be watched while these additional sounds are recorded and mixed into the track, is therefore an important facility. Here true artifice enters the work of the sound crew. Using tape recorders which can record and replay a considerable number of tracks simultaneously (a dozen or more is not uncommon) the crew can introduce new sounds, try them against alternatives, adjust the balance between one track and another, and re-record their final selection into a master soundtrack for evantual transfer to the film.

Speech, sound effects and music

While sound technicians have many other technical operations to perform if they are to record a clean and faithful track, the activities we have mentioned describe those points at which they exert the most creative control. We find again – as we found so often with lighting and camera work – that the crew have considerable opportunities to make creative choices which influence the way sound is perceived by the audience.

Three elements combine to build the soundtrack of a film. They are speech, sound effects and music.

Speech

The method of recording we described as we identified the principal items of equipment is by no means the only way of recording dialogue for a film. That particular method is conveniently referred to as 'direct sound' because it captures live action; and as we would expect from seeing how it works, it adds a certain quality of freshness to the event. This derives not only from its being live sound, but also from the difficulty the crew will experience recording in surroundings not prepared specifically for good acoustics. In other words there may be, for example, insufficient resonance, which would lead to a flat, dry sound; there might be excessive resonance, which would make for a booming effect. In addition, a certain amount of background noise (usually described as 'ambient sound') would be picked up.

These characteristics, which will suit certain kinds of screenplay, but not others, can be avoided by dubbing. By this method the words of the actors are recorded as they play for the camera: this recording is not intended for the final film but only as a 'guide track'. When the editor has cut the picture, the actors are recalled to dub. This they do by watching short segments of the film over and over again while the guide track plays through headphones to remind them of what they said and the rhythm of their words. When they have the phrasing of their lines in mind, they re-record their speech, matching their words to the lip movements on screen. It is a skilled business, and sufficiently demanding that it can rob the actor's voice performance of spontaneity – precisely the spontaneity that the direct sound method captures. However, it should be added that in some scenes as he performs for camera the actor has to concentrate so closely on his movement (to be in the right place for the lighting, looking in a planned direction, and moving on to some other precisely marked place), that he may not be able to give all the attention he would wish to what he says. In this case the additional polish he can provide by concentrating on voice only in the dubbing suite can allow him to improve his performance. Of course dubbing will also improve the quality of voice recording and will eliminate ambient noise.

It used to be the case that a film maker constructed his voice track either entirely by post-recording (dubbing) dialogue, or entirely by direct recording. When that was so, the more polished studio production would almost invariably opt for post-recording so that the balanced, well rounded quality of both performance and acoustics complemented the smooth movement of the cameras and total control of lighting. By contrast the rougher virtues of direct sound could suit and complement improvised acting, with location shooting and the use of lightweight, often handheld cameras. Thus post-recording tended to be associated with polished fictions, romantic comedies, dramas of many kinds; direct sound with socially conscious films, films of the French New Wave – that is films which attempted to preserve a sense of the actuality of people's lives.

More recently, however, relatively costly American feature films have used both methods, relying on direct sound for location work, exploiting the sense it conveys of an immediate, present reality and liberating their actors to improvise their lines. In short, the cinema of the big financial backers has chosen to mimic occasionally the appearance of the simple, intimate film. But it should be added that it imitates with a difference. The radio mikes which American productions rig for the direct recording of dialogue provide an altogether cleaner sound than the older methods of field recording; very little ambient sound is heard, and the voice is recorded without noticeable distortion. Thus direct voice tracks can be taken and mixed at a later stage with post-recorded effects tracks to make a composite soundtrack that combines the best of live sound and dubbed sound.

Dialogue has a central role in the creation of narrative; it is, put at its simplest, the means by which the characters of the plot express themselves. If dialogue were combined with the actions of the characters and everything else was excluded, the audience would still have a relatively plausible idea of what most films were about. We can check this by reading screenplays of films, for they give dialogue and stage directions, and relatively little else. This fact gives dialogue its massive authority in the soundtrack of most films. Indeed, if accompanied only by music and effects, most films would yield very little meaning.

The obvious authority of dialogue might lead us to think that it suffices that it should be spoken with vivid expression. While that is essential, we should also remember that directors cast not only for looks, but also for voice type. A director will not want two principal characters to sound alike for fear of giving rise to confusion. He also may wish to achieve some degree of characterisation through the qualities of each actor's voice – especially if he wishes to portray a type of character which is readily identifiable. This can be hard to make out in present day films: because we are so familiar with the voice types used they seem, often wrongly, to be natural. If we listen to an older movie, however, we quickly notice not only that the characters sound artificial, but that their voice patterns fall into distinct types: the gangster in a 1930s Hollywood thriller, for example, speaks with one kind of voice, the detective with quite another.

Sound effects

Direct sound

Like speech, sound effects can be recorded direct, or post-recorded. Direct sound will, as we have already learnt, incorporate into the finished track much more ambient noise than will an effects track that has been built piece by piece – and not all of that ambient sound will relate to the narrative. Although the direct recording can be mixed, the balance that a technician strikes on location will be altogether less subtle than that which can be achieved in the dubbing suite. One cause of this is that the sound engineer will find it more difficult to respond instantaneously to changes in level, or changes in the requirements of the scene which might call for level adjustments. The studio engineer can rehearse and try his mix before he finalises it. Secondly, direct sound is recorded after mixing on one track, and the balance of its constituent elements cannot be adjusted later. The only possible modification is to dub in 'wild sound' later (that is, sound recorded without the camera in operation), as a means of enriching what was originally taken. This is often done. A live track of, let us say, car engine noise is mixed with wild tracks of the same engine to give the finished soundtrack a smooth transition between shots that were probably recorded in different locations at different ranges from the machine.

For all these limitations, direct sound effects, like direct speech, have the advantage of intimacy. They seem to bring the audience close to the scene without the obvious intrusion of the full technology of a studio. The audience does not have to be aware of this consciously, but its reactions will be partly shaped by its sense of the way direct sound differs from studio sound.

Post-recorded effects

The same polished, high technology studio style can do for effects something comparable to what post-recording does for the voice. The effects track is built up from elements recorded independently for the particular segment of film for which they are intended. What are the advantages of this method over direct sound?

(1) *Balance.* A greater degree of sophistication can be achieved, dramatic enough for the listener to hear readily. The post-recording of sound effects usually builds the finished sound scene from elements recorded on separate tracks. So if our scene has sheep, people's footsteps, wind, and a passing car, the sound editor, having recorded all these items, can balance them according to the requirements of the script. That might call for the footsteps to be loudest, the wind very quiet, the sheep distant, and the car to fade in and then, after a brief moment of noisiness as it goes by, to fade out again. These distances will be aurally created in the dubbing suite to help give the picture its third dimension, so that what is seen as far off is heard as far off.

(2) *Selection.* The second advantage of post-recorded effects is that they can be selected according to the director's requirements. It has already been remarked that we hear selectively. The post-recording of sound enables the director to build his soundtrack so that we seem only to be listening to what we would be hearing in the same dramatic circumstances. Imagine a simple scene in which a young woman, after an exhausting day at work, returns home. As she goes through the door she is greeted by her children shouting, 'Mum! I'm hungry! When are we going to eat, Mum? Her husband, who has been home an hour, has prepared nothing, and sits comfortably watching television in the lounge. In actuality, in the urban streets in which most of us live there is

a considerable noise of traffic at rush hour; but in our film the director, to emphasise the young woman's weariness and isolation, may well keep that sound to the background in order to accentuate her footsteps as she walks from her car to the front door. Then, when she closes the door behind her, and although in life muted traffic would still be audible, the director would probably fade it entirely to concentrate attention on the family inside the house. In life, as the mother greets her children by the door, the television set would be audible; but for the moment she gives her attention to the children, and because she does not hear the set, the director keeps its noise out of our earshot too. Then, just as she begins to move through the house to look for her husband, that element of the soundtrack would be faded in to the middle ground.

These two elements, balancing and selection, give the post-recorded effects track a 'cleanness'. It has a rounder and clearer sound than the direct track; and unlike the direct track, which incorporates a number of 'redundant elements' (that is, sounds and noises which are on the track because the microphones picked them up, but which do not bear on the narrative), the post-recorded track is purpose built.

(3) *Sound modulation.* In one other vital aspect the post-recorded soundtrack has an advantage over the direct recording. That is in the creation of atmosphere or mood through the modulation of sound. Modulation simply means the varying of sound quality, and it can be done by a variety of means. An example will help make this clear. In an earlier chapter we imagined a train running down a long line of rail. Let us now think of this train blowing its horn, and place this event in three altogether different scenes:

(*a*) It is bringing the young and recently married hero and heroine back to their home town.

(*b*) An old woman and her husband watch the train passing from their country smallholding. They used to travel to the big cities which it connects, but now cannot afford to.

(*c*) A child is sitting on the line and is in danger of being crushed.

It is evident that the mood of these three scenes will be entirely different, but we will assume that the train is the same for each. It has only one horn, and in direct recording it would always sound the same, only louder or quieter according to the film makers' choice in live mixing. Now the variation of level or 'amplitude' of a sound is one of the variables in sound modulation, and it will be seen to be important in creating the mood of these three scenes. However, post-recorded sound can go further and vary the 'pitch' and *'timbre'* of effects. Amplitude can be changed at the turning of a knob. However, the modulation of either pitch (the frequency of the sound which makes it either a higher or lower note) or *timbre* (the blending of harmonics which gives a sound its harshness, sweetness or other character) are more complex adjustments. The key to the sound engineers' work lies in the fact that a post-recorded track will often be built from sounds that are not recorded from the objects on screen that appear to produce them. Not all our train sounds, then, will be produced by that train.

Sound engineers have a number of choices about how they proceed. In this instance they could have recorded a number of different locomotives 'wild' and dubbed these sounds onto the track as appropriate. They could have dubbed effects recorded in the studio – for the sound department will have a vast range of devices that create effects for a multitude of circumstances, and they might well have suitable horns. They could have dubbed the locomotive sound from a record of sound effects, for every studio builds its own library of stock sounds. Finally they could have created the sound electronically through a synthesiser; given the nature of the noise we have been considering, this would be an obvious way of proceeding for a crew that had a synthesiser at its disposal. The building of effects tracks can be accomplished by these several means to a sophisticated standard. Every kind of sound can be created in the studio and 'post-synched' (post-synchronised) to the action.

How, then, do our three scenes emerge from all this treatment?

(a) For this, the wedding scene, an atmosphere of celebration would be appropriate, and even the train's horn should match. It would sound loud and have a fairly high pitch to add to the cheerfulness of the scene. In addition it would have a clean, brassy *timbre* with no harshness about it.

(b) In this case the director wishes to create a mood of nostalgia and regret. To help achieve it he has the train's horn sound a somewhat lower pitch, and it is much quieter. As it passes the pitch drops in frequency, so that the sound is rather like a moan. Here the *timbre* of the sound is such as to give the effect of distance, not only in place, but also in time. A conventional way to achieve this through *timbre* is to give the sound a resonance that approaches an echo.

(c) Danger and fear are emotional keys to the last scene. Inevitably the horn must sound shockingly loud. The pitch of the note probably matters less than its *timbre*: this horn must positively blare. It will be at the furthest extreme imaginable from a smooth, honeyed tone, and will have an all but tangible harshness.

The artifice which goes into the creation of the post-recorded effects track raises the question of its claims to realism. The direct sound effects track, it will be recalled, guarantees the listener of its realism by its abundance of redundant elements (irrelevant traffic noise, indistinct voices and such sounds). The post-recorded track, by comparison, embodies only sounds that have dramatic purpose. Its faithfulness to actual life is always limited by the noises it leaves out. Its fidelity is to dramatic truth rather than to actuality; it is truth to the imagination over and above the outer world.

Music

Modulation

As in the analysis of effects, the observation of modulation helps us to appreciate the effects achieved by the music track. Indeed, the concept of modulation takes its origin from the analysis of music where a single, continuous sound may be modulated in terms of amplitude, pitch and *timbre*. We can imagine the one sustained sound, growing louder and softer, rising and falling in frequency and pitch, becoming harsh, then dry, perhaps then sweet, and finally resonant. Modulations in music in general can, of course, induce even more far-reaching effects, and if these changes are matched to a succession of dramatic moments, they can much enhance the spectator's reaction to what he sees.

It has sometimes been said that a higher pitch seems to increase tension, while a lower pitch is more relaxing. Statements of this kind can be true in given instances, but it is hard to generalise about the effects of modulation in quite so confident a way. What we can say, however, is that modulations in the music accompanying film can change our perception of the events portrayed in some way. We may be led to expect other things to happen, or we may be guided in our reponse to something that has just occurred. Either way our relation to the screen world is altered.

Rhythm

In general it is the rhythm of a piece of music that has the most irresistible impact on a sequence of film. From the technician's point of view we can say that it is virtually impossible to edit the images of a film successfully without making the rhythm of the cuts blend with the accompanying music's rhythm. From the spectator's point of view, the necessary thing to know is that the rhythm of accompanying music will take over and establish for us our sense of the pace of the scene which it accompanies.

This can be demonstrated by anybody with access to a videotape or an extract of film. It should be screened first with the original music on the soundtrack. Then it should be screened again with the sound turned off, and accompanied by music from another source – a gramophone or tape recorder. If this second piece of music has a tempo markedly different from the original, the effect on the perceived rhythm of the film is astonishing. A faster piece of music seems to speed it up, and conversely something more leisurely than the original slows it down. As analysts, then, we learn from this that, although music does not change the actual *speed* of events (action, camera movement, and cutting between shots) on screen, it provides us with a helpful guide to the *perceived pace* of those events.

Mood

As with its rhythm, the emotional colouring of music strongly affects the spectator's response to a scene. Commonly the music, whether 'motivated' or not (see below), so reinforces the scene that it sweeps up and embellishes its mood with vigour. In this aspect of music's impact we find that it possesses considerable authority in stamping scenes with its own characteristics.

However, music does not have to be restricted only to embellishing an established mood. Although a much less common effect, music can be used to distance the viewer from the visual subject. For instance, a scene can be constructed so that its music is identified as associated with a group with which we, seeing things from the point of view of the hero, do not sympathise. Perhaps a grief stricken hero, whom we favour strongly, comes upon a group of revellers dancing late into the night. The music of their dance fills the screen with good cheer. But his misery, and our attachment to it, contrast completely with the excitement of the dancers. The music 'leaves us cold'.

Motivated and interpretive music

It is convenient to classify music according to whether its presence in a scene arises directly from the screenplay (a character puts on a gramophone record, or attends a concert, or whatever), or whether it has no part in the drama acted out on screen, but has been added by the film maker to prompt his audience to interpret the scene in a particular way. The first kind is described as 'motivated music' because something that happens in the screenplay gives rise to music being heard. The second is 'interpretive music', its name describing its function.

Both kinds of music have the intense influence on our perception of the finished scene to which we have referred. It goes without saying that both kinds of music will have been carefully selected and inserted at the points at which they occur – there is nothing accidental about motivated music. And motivated music, just as much as interpretive, prompts the audience to make certain kinds of reading of the sequences it accompanies.

There was a time when interpretive and motivated music tended to differ quite markedly. By its nature as 'real' music which characters in a film listen to or play, motivated music has always had a certain independence within the image, and usually value in its own right. Until the mid 1960s interpretive music did not, in general, possess vivid enough qualities to give it interest in its own right. It was thought that it should function in support of narrative, and should not through its own elegance detract from it. Indeed, if we abstract our attention from the storyline of a commercial film made before that date, we will usually notice that the interpretive music is instructing the audience what to feel, and is not doing much else.

Interpretive music of this kind can be quite crude. The villains lie in wait to ambush the hero, and we hear a repeating series of unresolved, nervous chords on violins. He walks into the trap, and there follow three or four great crashes of brass and drums which end with the badmen attacking the hero. At this point the sound editor may employ the effect that silence can achieve at moments of crisis – for silence can often build tension and horror more effectively than roaring music. All too often, however, the producers insist on noise, and now, as the fists start flying the crashes of noise continue, synchronised to the landing of punches to heighten their impact.

To sit through an entire movie in which the music insists on our reacting this way or that can be an exhausting experience – and it has to be said that interpretive music is often written more tactfully. The impulse to use it extensively seems to have arisen from the fear on the part of production crews that their audiences needed this kind of prompt to be sure of enjoying themselves. Though some films are still accompanied by music of this kind, the American television series has become its true home in the years since the mid-1960s. Television producers know their dramas have to compete for attention with everything going on in the home. The producers of these series ruthlessly underline the action with such music so that people whose attention is split between the screen and something they are doing can keep in touch with the general trend of the plot.

Music composed to be heard in its own right will have a strong inner logic and consistency of its own. It may, for example, make certain thematic statements and develop them, and this will take time. In short, such music is not likely to adapt to punctuating each moment of an action. It follows that two possible functions of independent music of this kind are:

(a) to comment in a moment of quietness in the action either on what has just happened, or what is to come;
(b) to comment in a general way, rather than with detailed reference to the blow-by-blow progress of the plot, on what is currently happening.

Either way, the generalising nature of such music leaves the spectator with a measure of freedom in which to form his own judgment. It is not as insidiously directive as music written specifically for film can be.

Pre- and post-recorded music

The differences between motivated and interpretive music are present even in the way they are recorded. Motivated music will usually be recorded before the film is shot, that is pre-recorded. It may be taken from a record that is already in circulation; or it may be released in record form as an additional source of income tied to the opening of the film. In either of these cases pre-recording has taken place, and if the characters are supposed to play or sing, they mime to the disc. This technique is almost always called on in the preparation of musicals: performers have more than enough to cope with in mastering their dance routines without having to record a perfect song at the same time, and as the music has to exist for them to dance to, post-recording is not economical.

Occasionally a performer will record live, but this is relatively unusual as the balancing of acoustics for music requires a more carefully controlled aural environment than does speech. The technical problems are considerable.

By contrast interpretive music is usually post-recorded. It is not hard to understand why. Given that it is to sway our feelings about the scenes it accompanies, a score that comments on screen action would be impossibly demanding on the film makers if it pre-existed the shooting of a film. There are many points in a film where the mismatch of only a second between music and action would be a calamity. Take a standard scene from a thriller: three shots ring out and a man dies. The three shots are to be followed immediately by an orchestral crash. Now if that sound arrived early, it would precede the shots, which would be absurd. If it came late by a second, it would have a subtly different effect: instead of emphasising the shots themselves, the chord would now, after this short interval, stress what they have done. The meaning of musical punctuation changes just through its timing alone, and it would now emphasise the horror of the death that the shots have caused.

Thus when interpretive music integrates with action as closely as this, it would be virtually impossible to record it before the shooting of the film. The actors' and crew's work would have to be timed to an exactitude that would make them move like marionettes. In practice, music of this kind is frequently only written when all the rest of the film is complete. The composer then has the film before him as he works, and can time his score exactly to the requirements of the screen drama. In his turn the conductor leading the recording orchestra paces his musicians to match the action, which he does by keeping an eye on a replay of the movie as they record.

Sound and film composition

Synchronous and wild sound

Synchronous sound is that which some event on screen causes. Someone opens his mouth, and as the lips move we hear speech. He crosses the room and we hear footsteps. Wild sound, sometimes called 'asynchronous sound', is everything else.

In the earliest days of the sound film it seemed logical to film makers that the soundtrack should include sounds made by nothing that was not seen; and that everything which was in view that would in life be heard should be on the soundtrack. That is to say, their ideal was to record a very full synchronous track, on the grounds that this would be the most lifelike thing to do. However, as we have already learnt, hearing works selectively, so we can appreciate readily that such a soundtrack, reproducing all the effects possible, would be heavily congested. Film makers discovered this quickly too. Having learnt to select sounds, they continued for a while to reproduce only synchronous sound, that is only sound that, so to speak, could be seen. This turned out to be a boring way to treat it; they soon realised the attractions of wild sound and began to incorporate it. There are both physiological and artistic reasons for wanting to do so.

As Reisz and Millar point out, hearing has the advantage over sight that we receive signals from all directions, whereas our eyes see only those things they point towards. In effect we hear, and are oriented towards what we cannot see: movement behind us, traffic over the horizon, music in the next room. Wild sound can provide the film's equivalent for this kind of experience.*

Thus wild sound exploits for cinema the fact that we hear by a different channel from that through which we see. If the soundtrack confirms what the eyes can see, this can be a helpful and reassuring function; but beyond a certain point it simply provides redundant information – redundant because we already have it. However, the concept of redundant information is slightly more complicated than this, for though we receive the cinema's signals via two channels, the eyes and the ears, we do so through five quite different coding systems which do not all reduplicate each other. They are (1) visual images, (2) written language (titles, letters, newspaper headlines etc.), (3) speech, (4) sound effects, and (5) music. Thus if we see someone speak, to hear what he is saying does not reduplicate to the point of redundancy the information provided by the images; rather it satisfies a need as visual images cannot codify the detail of dialogue. The most obvious

*Karel Reisz & Gavin Millar *The Technique of Film Editing*, (Focal Press, London, 2nd ed, 1968, pp.256ff.

redundancy occurs when sound effects needlessly reduplicate what the narrative has already expressed through other coding systems (visual images, speech, and perhaps music). Discussing earlier the over-emphatic use of interpretive music we were in effect describing another clear form of redundancy.

The ways in which wild and synchronous sound enhance information carried by images are now altogether more sophisticated than they were in the early years of the sound film, and their conscious application has consequences for the control of space and time in the film. We will deal briefly with these topics in turn.

Sound and space: composition in the frame

What we hear can affect the way we see. A film maker can reorganise his picture not only according to the visual principles we investigated in Part 3, but also according to the way he builds his soundtrack.

On-screen space

If two or more people are in frame and one talks to the others, he will tend to attract the attention of viewers. So long as the speeches are terse, we will tend to look at the speaker; but if the character goes on a bit, we usually find ourselves looking away for more information, and in particular to know how his listeners are taking what he says. (It is still the case that if someone makes a bold movement, that will catch our eyes.)

Composition of the image around speakers is only one way sound can centre visual attention. Effects can do it too. Imagine the following example. In a widescreen production two characters are deep in conversation at the extreme left of the screen. Suddenly an unexpected noise is heard (let us say the click of a rifle bolt locking home), and either a very small movement in the shrubbery to the right of the screen, or the fact that the two actors swing round to gaze at that point, reveals to us the source of the noise. (Only in a few cinemas is sound actually directional, and for that reason the audience needs these clues to where it comes from.) Our attention swings right across the screen, and the director has effectively recomposed his image with a sound, for scarcely anything has happened pictorially.

Sound has another important function in contributing to our sense of on-screen space. It adds substantially to our sense of the third dimension, depth. A sound made by someone or thing in the foreground will differ both in amplitude and *timbre* from the same sound in the middleground, and differ again from the sound in the background. Typically, while the level falls, resonance might be increased with distance. Thus the work of the sound engineer complements that which the lighting and camera crew do to create an illusion of depth.

To say this much is to remark only upon the thoroughly familiar. There is, however, an interesting variation on this pattern, itself a convention, which has attracted little notice – yet it reveals an aspect of the relation between the audience and the screen event in a novel way. What happens is that a long, or an extreme long shot of a character is coupled to an intimate close-up of his voice. The apparent contradiction does not seem that way to the audience, which reads this particular picture/sound combination as something natural. It seems so because it fulfils the audience's desire to feel specially privileged in its knowledge of principal characters – so this device becomes not a means of cheating space as much as a method of creating a strong sense of subjectivity.

Off-screen space

Wild sound extends our knowledge of what is happening beyond the confines of the picture frame. Imagine an establishing shot of a living room in which some action to which we are giving our attention is taking place. In the background there is an open window, but the camera is so placed that we cannot see anything through it. On the soundtrack there is a constant rumble of heavy traffic. We are in town. Change the soundtrack so that birdsong replaces the traffic, and we are in the country.

In that instance sound is the only means of establishing off-screen space. It also functions as one of a number of indicators about what is happening out of sight when the picture is cutting between a number of angles. If a character walks out of frame, but continues to talk to someone still in frame we have the soundtrack to tell us something about where he is. That information will often be reinforced by the eyeline of the actor in frame who may well be looking at him. If he keeps on talking, the editor will probably cut to a fresh angle of him, and now the listener will be off-screen, located only by the visual information provided by the speaker's eyeline until he begins to answer.

Sound and time

Film is a medium which operates both in space and time. If dealing with wild sound we have referred only to its capability to position events in space, that does not mean that the time dimension is absent. As it is, we have been dealing with simultaneous events and have not moved out of the present. It is possible, however, for sound to refer to a different time period from that of the images. Where, for example, a narrator relates what he has seen, he speaks in the present about events seen and now acted out in a fictional past; or in the flashback, the image cuts back to past time, but the soundtrack, for a while at least, remains in the present. These devices are well established; but there is another which originated in the work of the more adventurous European directors of the late

1950s and early 1960s. When one scene ends and the next begins the soundtrack cuts first, and the picture some seconds later. For a while the old scene is watched while the new one, often rather puzzlingly, is heard over it. Though the device was originally intended to surprise audiences into a new awareness of what was happening on screen, it has since become familiar and rather less arresting through repetitious use. None the less, undoubtedly one of the most exciting prospects for future film experiment lies in playing with the time bond between image and soundtrack.

From these observations we can develop the concept of sound running in counterpoint to the image. While parallel or synchronous sound is essential to the expression and comprehension of the narrative, what might be called 'contrapuntal sound' refers to everything that has its source out of the frame – that is, everything from interpretive music, to the voice of a narrator, the sounds of people in rooms off-screen, the voices of people in another country and the next scene, or of people from a remembered past or a desired future. It can be readily understood, then, that contrapuntal sound has done more than help the cinema towards its extraordinary freedom to move in space and time: it also allows it to move in ways which are normally the exclusive property of the imagination.

Part 5

Editing

EVERY ASPECT OF THE CINEMATIC PROCESS that we have considered has been found to transform those elements of the actual world on which it works into cinematic material. Editing in turn works on those transformed materials and changes them further. Thus the cinema's marvellous distortion of reality reaches perfection in the editing process.

In its essence what happens at the editing table can be easily enough reduced to a simple formulation. For the editor sees and hears all the material that has been shot and recorded for the film. From this mass of material he selects the footage that is to be included and assembles the film. If he discovers that a scene lacks either certain shots or necessary sound, he may also advise the director to shoot additional material.

The editor's work can be reduced in outline to the linked tasks of selecting and assembling filmic material, but this is both a challenging and a creative job. It challenges the editor not least because of the complexity and size of the process: there may be ten times as much film as will finally be used, and the finished soundtrack may be built from hundreds of items to be mixed from perhaps twenty separate tracks. Just how the editor organises this mass of material it is not our business to study. We shall restrict ourselves to examining the finished film to find what effects editing has brought about, and to see some of the typical patterns of cutting the viewer meets again and again.

The film is put into its final form in the editing room, and it is this process that gives the cinema its extraordinary dynamism and dramatic freedom. On their tables editors can bring together shots and sounds from very different places and times. Simply by cutting and joining lengths of film and tape (the first editors actually worked with scissors and glue and little else), they can instantaneously switch the audience from today back hundreds of years or forward into the imagined future. Equally the editor can shift from one continent to another or to a place, realised in a studio, that exists only in the imagination.

The functions of editing

The editor undertakes four different, though overlapping classes of operation.*

*I owe this division of the subject to Ralph Stephenson and J. R. Debrix, *The Cinema as Art*, Penguin Books, Harmondsworth, 2nd edn, 1970, pp.69–72.

1. *Changing the scene*

In the way we have just described, cutting can change the scene in accordance with the requirements of the script, concluding the action in one scene, and introducing a new one which may take place in another place, or time, or both. Such changes may be as dramatic as those mentioned above, or they may be subtle: two characters finish a conversation, and one enters the next room and talks to someone else.

2. *Omission*

We have already mentioned that in the process of editing a great deal has to be left out, using as an absurd example the idea of a film about the life and times of some famous person. The audience will not expect to sit for seventy years. For all its absurdity the thought helps us recognise that the editing process begins long before a foot of film is turned. Though the culmination of that process takes place on the editor's bench, it begins on the scriptwriter's desk. The script itself represents a substantial exercise in editing, and a good scriptwriter has among his talents the skill to choose which episode will make a point tellingly, and which can be left out without robbing the screenplay of an essential dramatic development.

Working on this large scale, then, both the scriptwriter and the editor (who may in turn leave out episodes that had been filmed for inclusion) will be trying to cut out all scenes but those which reveal something that the audience at a given point in the drama need to know. A scene which would have been informative at the beginning of a film may turn out to be quite wasted at a later stage if it does not add to what has already been revealed, and turn the drama into new channels. If they happen to be making a 'Life-and-times' film the writer and editor might well go for those episodes in the life which changed the character, emphasising the person he is becoming rather than his present state of being. That is not a rule; but it is convenient for dramatic ends that the subject of a biography should be seen to change.

How much the editor can omit from a story depends on how familiar he believes his audience to be with the kind of film he is constructing. It is evident that well-known genres such as westerns or thrillers can today be told with economy because the audience know roughly where they are going. But the spectator who has been out of touch with that particular kind of film for a number of years, like the parent taking his children to the movies after years of absence, can experience a problem. He may not at once grasp everything that is going on between the shots: information that has been cut out.

The other aspect of omission worth mentioning here is the requirement that the editor has to select from much more material than he could possibly use for any given scene. The crew will have shot perhaps ten times as much as will be built into the film. The editor has to decide which take best conveys the dramatic point the scene should make. He will have other choices to make too, and these, together with the ways in which he omits smaller units of time, are dealt with later (pages 112–21).

3. *Varying the point of view*

By bringing together shots taken from different points within the scene the editor completes the process, which again should have begun with the scriptwriter, of responding to the audience's desire to change its point of view. This, it will be recalled, (pages 58–60) does more than just refresh the eye with variety, though it does that too. The control of point of view puts the viewer in some particular relation to the film text, making him, for instance, party to what is going on (subjective p.o.v.); a dispassionate observer (objective p.o.v.); or the privileged spectator of a narrative which unfolds for his benefit alone (privileged p.o.v.).

4. *Building a mental image or idea*

The assembly of a number of shots can trigger the audience into creating mental pictures of things which they never see on the screen in their entirety. Such 'things' can be either places or events. This principle of assembly can be extended so that ideas are created by the relationship between shots rather than anything in the shots themselves.

A mental picture of a place can be built up by the viewer from the information he gets in a number of close shots. It is not uncommon for a room, say, never to be shown in a master shot, but to be covered in a variety of angles, the principal subjects of which are the actors moving in the room. The audience builds its own image of the entire room from the fragments it sees. An extension of this method puts the audience in the position of assembling for itself a place that never existed. For example, a film may take place in a house, but, in shooting, the crew may find the best locations are the exterior of one house, interiors from two others, and a kitchen scene which has been shot on a studio set. The audience, if the dramatic action assures them that everything is taking place in one house, will build what it sees into a complete house that exists nowhere except in their imaginations.

A similar method of construction builds certain kinds of event, particularly those which are dangerous. A man falls into an African river and is chased by a crocodile. After swimming desperately with the reptile closing in on him, he manages to clamber ashore just out of reach of the creature's jaws, and is saved. As actors cannot be killed off lightly, and crocodiles have unreasonable appetites, it would be normal practice in filming such an adventure to keep the crocodile and the performer apart. The editor and the audience between them create the scene. First the camera crew take a number of shots of the actor falling in the water, swimming frantically, looking over his shoulder, screaming, shouting for help. Then with the actor safely out of the way, they take another set of shots from matching angles of an angry and active crocodile. And they add to these a set of reaction shots of people on the banks of the river gasping, crying out, hiding their eyes, running up and down. The editor 'intercuts' these shots so that we switch back and forth from seeing the man to looking at his deadly pursuer, and across to the horrified onlookers whose reaction adds to our tension. As the pursuit goes on, the editor cuts the component shots shorter and shorter, and the effect is of accelerated pace, and a shortening of the distance between reptile and man.

It has to be said that this version would by today's standards of editing compile a rather simple chase, and it would be more common to add master shots with horribly convincing model crocodiles chasing the unfortunate actor or a stunt stand-in. In addition, the pace of cutting would be more varied than suggested above. None the less, classic Hollywood has many examples of scenes created in the minds of the audience from materials just as limited as these: there have been far too many crocodile chases constructed in just this way.

The creation of an idea can proceed by means as simple as those called on to create an event. The famous experiments conducted by Lev Kuleshov serve as an example. He intercut a neutral, inexpressive close-up of a man with shots of various objects; the shot of the man was unchanging. The other shots included a bowl of soup, a coffin, and a little girl at play. In each case it appeared to the audience that the actor was looking at the object. They saw him as expressing in the first instance hunger, with the second shot, grief, and lastly happiness. In actuality these emotions had been read by the audience as a consequence of connections they made between the coupled shots, neither of which had the meaning they drew from them. The audience had produced new meaning from the collision between these separate elements.

That viewers do connect a series of shots and draw meaning from them in this way can be confirmed by those scenes in which a change in the running order of the shots would change the meaning.

(1) A man looks serious.
(2) He reads a letter.
(3) He now looks happy.

Run in that order, the scene tells us that the letter brings good news. If the same three shots should be cut together in the reverse order, the letter contains bad news.

As with other aspects of cinema, so too editing is governed by conventions rather than rules. These conventions have authority for a time, often for quite a long time, but eventually someone finds an alternative pattern, and the old convention lapses as a new one takes its place. It is useful, therefore, to begin to look at some of the conventions of cutting and assembling narrative films which have become familiar in the cinema of the West. We will start with the methods of linking film – the punctuation marks, so to speak – as they are the most visible marks of the editing process.

Methods of linking shots

The cut

This is the commonest means of making the transition between one shot and the next, and is the simplest mechanically. The film is literally cut; the end of the first shot is trimmed to the chosen length, the start of the second shot is selected and trimmed, and the two lengths of film are joined. The effect is of an immediate transition from one shot to the next. This transition may be abrupt or sᵣ ooth, but this quality depends on the logic of the relationship between the two shots rather than on the cut itself. We shall pursue this topic when we deal with continuity.

The fade

This is exactly what its name suggests: the image either 'fades in' from a blank screen by a progressive change in which the picture gradually reveals itself; or it 'fades out' through the converse progression from a complete image back to a blank screen. The most familiar convention-alised function of fades is to indicate the beginning and end of scenes. It also occurs as a sign that the scene in the film represents only part of what happened.

The dissolve

The dissolve may be described as the superimposition of a fade out and a fade in. The impression is of an image dissolving into or mixing with another, with the second image emerging as the new shot after a brief period in which the two are superimposed one upon the other. Until the early 1960s, in its most familiar usage the dissolve indicated the passage of a period of time between one scene and the next. However, since the work of the French New Wave gained currency, it has come to serve in more varied ways. If it deals at all with time it may imply the omission of time within an ongoing scene. (Time transitions since the New Wave have more commonly been indicated by cutting to show that time elapses *between* scenes, the sense of time passing being signalled both by the narrative and the rhythm of the film.) Other new functions of the dissolve include indicating some kind of thematic links between two scenes. An emotional link between scenes may also be implied by the same means.

The wipe

One image can appear to supplant another by wiping it off the screen. In its simple form the wipe appears as a line that moves across the screen; in doing so, it progressively conceals the first image as it reveals the new one. Unlike the 'push-off' (see below), the subjects of each image remain static in relation to the frame.

Wipes can also take a variety of complex forms, particularly in electronic variants for television: wipes that spiral, zigzag, or assume expanding geometrical shapes are all common.

Other devices
Several devices long out of fashion are now returning to currency through electronic effects-generators in television studios. They include the *iris* in which the image opens out from a point in the frame, and closes down to a point at the end of the scene. There is the *turnover* in which the image appears to roll, and as it does so another takes its place. Then in the *push-off* one incoming image seems to push the outgoing one off the screen. All of these devices were popular in cinema at various times from the 1920s to the 1940s. In common with the wipe, they draw attention to themselves and make the transition between shots noticeable. In television they often mark the transition between items within a single programme. In narrative film they provide ornate markers between one scene and the next. They would, however, interrupt story continuity needlessly and so do not find much use within a continuing scene.

Continuity

Given that the finished film will have been built from a multitude of pieces of film and tape, there is every possibility for its final appearance to be highly fragmentary. This may be the effect the film maker desires; but usually in a narrative feature film he will want to create the illusion of a flowing and uninterrupted tale. Either way, the film will have been contrived carefully in order to produce the effect it does; and the crew will have had to consider its continuity. Continuity refers to the relationship between shot and shot. 'Classic continuity' refers to the style of film making that seeks to give the illusion of smooth and self-sufficient completeness of the kind that Hollywood has mastered for so long. Contrasted to it are various discontinuous or dislocating styles of film cutting.

For convenience, continuity may be analysed according to three aspects, though they inevitably interconnect. They are the control of *sequencing*, of *space*, and of *time*.

The control of sequencing

This entails the preservation in the relationship between shots of the intended logic of the screenplay. It is the aspect of continuity which receives the most popular attention, but it holds relatively little interest for the analyst as it reveals little about the purposes of the crew or the meaning of the film.

Since the film is assembled from shots taken at many times and places, seldom in the order of the script, errors in the relationship between shots can easily occur unless the crew observe careful control over this aspect of their work. Where that control fails an actor might, in walking from one room to the next, leave the first shot dressed in a suit, and enter the second in sports clothes. Or his cigarette might be longer in the second shot than in the first. The control of sequencing has to extend beyond guarding against absurdities of this kind to making sure lighting, sets, costumes, props, the position and movements of actors all follow as intended from one shot to the next.

The control of space

The reference grid by which the audience orients itself to action on the screen is the frame. For the editor this means that the fragments of space captured in successive shots cannot be assembled totally at random if the audience is to continue to know where it is. The editor – and the camera crew and director before him – is likely to relate his work to the *centre line* and the *eyeline* to control space in a manner that has become familiar. Once again it needs to be said that respect for centre lines and eyelines as conventions is not an essential component of film making; but where they are ignored, they must be substituted with alternative patterns of spatial logic if the audience is to know how to relate one shot to the next.

The centre line

The centre line is sometimes known as the 'line of action'; and its application as a guide to camera placement is often known as the '180° rule'. If two characters talk together, the line which could be drawn between them is the centre line. Where a character walks along, his path constitutes the line of action. What the 180° rule says is that the camera may only be placed to one side of this line if the characters are to remain on the same sides of the screen that they started, and to continue to move in the same direction.

It is easy to see what happens when the centre line is crossed. Imagine two people in conversation. Look at them from one side and A is on the left, B on the right. Cross to the other side of them and B now occupies the left position, A the right. Now if you try this in life you will see what is meant, but the effect is not confusing because you know where you are. In the cinema, however, the screen is your only point of reference since your seat does not move; so if two characters switch places without motivation, it does tend to bring about a sharp visual discontinuity.

The same observations may be made about camera coverage of movement. A person shot from the left as he walks along is seen moving, say, from left to right. Cross to the other side of the line of action, and his direction of movement is now seen as right to left. To the spectator who is not cued to expect this kind of movement it may appear that the character has turned round and is going back the way he came.

It is worth following the logic of the 'rule' to its most rigorous conclusion, as this shows at their most demanding the requirements the editor has to fulfil when establishing logical space. Since the camera can move freely from point to point on its chosen side of the line, it may be said to have open to it a hemisphere of movement. However, this broad angle of movement shrinks markedly if a third person is introduced into a conversation, and the camera looks between two characters standing close together at the third. Now almost any movement will take it across a centre line, for it would seem logical to extend similar lines between each of the three characters, and the camera is thus caught between two of them. Jammed into this tiny segment of the floor, how can the editor move his shot to another angle?

Actually the trap is not as complete as it seems. The line has to be crossed. The first choice open to the editor is to cross it precisely in such a way that the characters shift places in a manner that causes the spectator a surprise. In other words he violates the 'rule' and reverses the characters on screen. If however he wants to make a smooth transition between shots, he has to employ some other means. There are plenty of options available and they can do much to enhance the spatial elegance of the film. Some of these have nothing directly to do with the editor. For example, the director can ask his actors to move in shot; as they do so the audience sees new spatial relationships set up, and of course is not disoriented. Alternatively the camera itself may be moved during the shot, and once again the audience sees where it is going.

However, the editor will often want to cut across a centre line, and to do so smoothly he has to bring about some kind of visual distraction so that the audience forgets where the old centre line used to be. These devices can only be brought into play if they have been thought of before shooting takes place. Editing is once again seen to have essential roots in pre-planning. Here are four ways of cutting across the centre line:

(1) From a tight group shot, the editor can cut back to a wide *establishing shot*. Holding this for a few seconds will enable viewers to forget their former orientation, and it is then possible to cut in to a new tight group shot which violates the former line.

(2) The editor can cut to a *neutral shot*, a shot in which the principal character of the moment is either looking or moving directly towards or away from the camera. Again, after a few seconds the editor can cut to a

new position across the old centre line, and the audience's recollection of the first shot will be distant enough for it not to experience disorientation.

(3) A *bridging shot* can be cut in. There are two kinds, the 'insert' and the 'cutaway'. Bridging shots are shots of a fresh subject cut into an ongoing action. While they should be informative, and reveal to the audience something useful for it to know, they also have the advantage that they provide yet another form of visual distraction to the audience, after which the centre line can be crossed.

The 'insert' presents an image of a detail of the scene which has some particular dramatic significance for the moment. A person is threatened and looks about for a handy weapon; his eye lights upon a kitchen knife. Cued by the actor's look, the camera cuts in to a detail insert of the knife, and then cuts out again to resume coverage of the action between villain and innocent. In cutting out to the third shot, the editor can cross the line between the two characters. As this example shows, inserts are extremely useful in providing additional information; their function in crossing the line should be secondary in importance.

The 'cutaway' differs from the insert in that it is a shot of some thing or action not a part of the original scene. That thing or action will, though, be related, otherwise it would have no place in the script. As a device for crossing the line, plainly it is a most effective distraction. It has narrative functions too, one of the most familiar being to act as an equivalent for what in the novel is introduced by the word 'meanwhile'. In a busy office an angry manager shouts at his secretary. Meanwhile (cutaway shot) a traffic warden gums a ticket to the window of his car which is illegally parked outside. The event happening meanwhile may prove to be worth developing into an intercut sequence in which the camera shifts back and forth between that scene and this. That pattern, of which the chase is the famous example, is called 'parallel development' (see page 117), and it often begins with a cutaway.

(4) *The reaction shot*, like the bridging shots, has an essential narrative role. It guides the audience in its emotional response to the action by presenting it with an image of one or more characters reacting to what they have seen. Thus the reaction shot will very often feature a secondary player responding to some drama involving a principal. This secondary player draws the audience's response because it has the chance to see someone else's emotional reaction to circumstances they have all been through. Clearly a shot of this power is sufficient distraction also to allow the line to be crossed unnoticed.

It is also actually possible for an editor in certain circumstances to cut directly across the line without the audience noticing it. This practice is better understood when we know how 'eyeline matching' works.

The eyeline

This simply refers to the direction of gaze of an actor. While it may often coincide with the centre line, when for instance two characters speak to each other, it may also diverge, as when the same two characters hear a knock at the door and look in that direction.

The significance to the editor of the characters' eyelines lies in their role in defining off-screen space. A and B talk to each other. In the master shot A is to the left of screen looking right, B to the right looking left. When the editor cuts in to a close shot of either of them, he will need them still to be looking in much the same screen direction, for if B should now look out of frame right instead of left, he would appear to have turned around and to be looking in the same direction as, rather than at A. Thus the eyeline of the visible character defines the off-screen position of the one out of shot.

Eyeline movement is often used to direct the audience's attention. Our two characters in conversation hear a noise. They look round at the source of the noise, and if they look at a point within the frame, we follow their glance towards it. If they look out of the frame, their glance cues the editor to cut to an insert that reveals the source of the sound.

Eyeline movement operates with subtlety in creating and switching centre lines in larger groups. Earlier the notion was mooted that between three characters there must be three centre lines, and that the camera, without the aid of distractions to help it cross them, would be badly trapped. Actually, it would have been more accurate to refer to *potential* centre lines. Only one is likely to dominate at any given time – the *dominant* centre line. This circumstance arises from the familiar practice in narrative drama whereby only one character speaks at a time. The speaker's eyeline forms the centre line that dominates, and often it will be directed at only one of the other two. The third character is for the moment subordinate, but he plays a necessary role, for at a certain point as the dialogue between the other two continues, he switches his gaze from the one he has been watching to the other. Cued by his shift of attention, the camera switches to an alternative point of view, and so long as it does so without breaking the dominant centre line between the other two characters, the audience is not likely to be much disturbed. What happens is that the two characters locked in conversation will stay in the same spatial relation, left and right of each other. The third character, who cued the cut, will be switched by it to an unexpected part of the screen, probably remote from where he was; but the audience is still giving most of its attention to the other two, and so barely notices.

No book, let alone a short introduction to the subject, can hope to classify the many subtle variations of movement between shot and shot.

Fuller accounts can be found elsewhere, and these may be consulted for a somewhat more detailed investigation of the possibilities.*

We need now to give some thought to the effects of respecting centre and eye lines. As we have seen, by observing these conventions the editor can build from a series of shots an imaginary space, the relationship of the parts of which is logical and well ordered. We seem to be looking at segments of a continuous space within the bounds of any given scene. As we have already learnt (page 101) this is not by any means always the way things were in front of the camera, but that it appears to be so on the screen contributes to the kind of self-contained illusion that the style known as 'classic continuity editing' builds up. We shall see more fully how this style works when we deal with editing and time.

For the moment it is enough to remember that the building of seemingly continuous space is only one way of approaching the editor's task. There are circumstances in which the editor deliberately tries to fragment space, and here he will purposely cross the centre line, mismatch his eyelines, violating these conventions for conscious reasons. Often this is done to draw attention to the film as a film, and to break the perfection of the illusion. If a director has characters in separate shots speaking to each other, and in terms of the conventions we have been describing they are obviously not looking at each other; if he has them moving about a room whose parts appear rather to break asunder than to come together; if as they move they seem to alter direction illogically – then the effect on an audience used to the continuous and co-ordinated handling of space will be marked. Such an audience will perceive the breakdown of a familiar order clearly. That was, to return to an example cited earlier (pages 97–8), the effect of the changes to the coding of cinematic space which the directors of the New Wave brought to the European cinema of the 1960s. The effect, fresh to cinema of the day, was at times comparable to the Brechtian process of making the familiar seem strange – of making the audience look with new eyes at what was deliberately presented to it as an artifice. Audiences, however, familiarise themselves swiftly with new patterns of coding information. It is noticeable, for instance, that American Cinema of the New Wave era (that is the cinema of the young directors of the 1970s, who adopted the European name) uses methods of space and time fragmentation borrowed from that European model. Yet they do so without inconveniencing their audiences or discarding the self-containing cinematic illusion. Crossing the line, for instance, is a lot less visible and intrusive a thing to do than it used to be, simply because the audience has got used to it.

*Daniel Arijon's *Grammar of the Film Language*, Focal Press, London, 1976, is as detailed a classification as any, and the idea of the dominant centre line is one he develops at length.

The control of time

We have already had occasion to note that any narrative film will leave out more than it keeps in. Even in the scripting process huge expanses of time are excluded, and only certain moments in the lives of the characters are covered. Beyond this stage of editing the script between scenes, the scenes themselves can be edited in such a way as to control the passage of film time within them. On the editing bench time can be stretched or shrunk.

This is best understood if we first have a grasp of the principal methods of shooting entire sequences. These are termed 'cover shooting' and 'overlapping action'.

Cover shooting

This will occur where the director decides, without any fixed idea where the cuts will fall, to provide the editor with very free choice. He 'covers' the action first from a master shot, and then from a number of closer positions, getting his performers to replay all or substantial parts of the sequence. Thus for any given moment in the script the editor may have in front of him a master establishing shot, a two-shot, and one or more close shots. There may be other shots besides, and, of course, he will in fact have several takes of each, most with flaws, but usable in part. He has to choose both which take of which shot to select for any given moment, and when to cut into and out of it. Cover shooting is costly in that it consumes a great deal of film, and requires actors to render several satisfactory performances of each scene. While it gives greater freedom to the editor, it can result in rather unoriginal camera work because the basic positions for this kind of work are familiar from countless such scenes.

Overlapping action

This reduces the freedom of the editor because much of the script will be covered by one shot only, though here too there may be several usable takes of each shot. The director has an approximate idea of where he wants the cuts to fall before he runs the camera. He shoots rather more than he thinks necessary to make those cuts, starting each shot earlier than he wants to cut in, and ending it later than the proposed moment of cutting away from it. When the same procedure is followed with every shot the editor finds he has an overlap between shots, and his cut must fall somewhere in that overlapped section. Compared to cover shooting, overlapping action is cheaper on film, less demanding on the actors, and can bring about a more imaginative use of cameras because every shot has to be thought of in relation to the one before and after it – no single shot runs for the duration of the entire sequence, as it would with cover shooting.

Whichever method has been employed, the editor has before him more footage than he needs; among other opportunities, this gives him the chance to decide for every shot how to co-ordinate the passing of time between it and the shot that follows. This process is called the 'articulation of time'.

The articulation of time

In his useful analysis of the ways two shots can be related in time, Noël Burch divided all the possible relationships into five classes.*

(1) The two shots may be *perfectly continuous*, the action at the end of the first shot being continued without interruption in the second. Burch cites the instance of a person going through a door, shot first from one side and then the other. The cut is made so that the movement is shown in its entirety, and continuity is preserved with a sense of real time being observed.

(2) There may be a *measurable time abridgement* between the two shots. In other words a short period of time of a recognisable length could have been cut out. It is commonplace for narrative film to avoid showing all of an action when it is not significant. Cutting out the insignificant part has the effect of speeding up the action and concentrating attention on those parts of the story which are intended to convey meaning. In this case the person passing through the door might be shown reaching it and turning the handle, then the shot might cut to the second angle which begins with his completing the closing of the door behind him. The actual movement through the door is eliminated. Provided the action cut out would have been continuous, the abridgement or shortening is measurable. This is not the case with the next kind of abridgement.

(3) In an *indefinite time abridgement* the only clue to how much time has passed can be found in external things – change of clothes, of seasons, of light, or of a calendar. This kind of time abridgement, which usually embraces longer periods of time, relates closely to the gaps left in the narrative by the screen writer. At the end of one scene a character may say that he will go to see someone, and at the start of the next he meets that person. Just how much time, whether minutes or months, has elapsed, we can tell only from external information, for the time cut out is itself discontinuous – that is, it covers more than one single, measurable event.

(4) With *measurable time reversal* part of an action which should be continuous is repeated. Used nakedly this device disrupts the audience's sense of real time, and establishes a time scale which is uniquely cinematic. If our character going through a door is shown at the end of the first shot almost through it, and then at the start of the next back at the point where he is about to open it, a deliberate dislocation takes

*Noël Burch *Theory of Film Practice*, Secker & Warburg, London, 1973, pp.4–8.

place which draws attention to the action, and also extends time as a part of the action is repeated. The film also draws attention to its own mechanisms since we do not experience time in this way in any other circumstances. This device was much used in this disruptive way by Sergei Eisenstein; and lately the films of Nicolas Roeg have made a feature of it.

There is, however, an altogether more commonplace practice of time reversal, which might be described as *concealed time reversal*. In this case the point of overlap between the two shots is disguised, usually by the choice of a moment to cut when an action, which does not have a definite time dimension, is taking place. If a character is shown raising his arm to drink, any measurable time reversal of that movement cannot but be observed, as the dimensions of that movement have limits which we all know. But where a character is walking along a passage, repeated overlap cutting of his movement from a variety of different angles may be undiscoverable. If we do not know how long the corridor was in actuality, it is transformed by the editing process to be as long as it takes to walk down it – provided always the camera does not reveal the full length of it in a single shot. In such a case both time and space stretch, and the corridor grows longer to the viewer than it was to the actor.

(5) Finally Burch refers to the *indefinite time reversal*, where we go back a period in time that cannot be measured because it is not a part of a continuous action. Again external clues are the only indicators of how much time has been returned over. As Burch points out, the commonest appearance of this particular type of time articulation is found in the flashback, where the film cuts back to an event that happened some period before the scene just concluded. Flashback is a scripted device; as with indefinite time abridgement, indefinite reversal corresponds often to shifts planned in the screenplay.

Editing styles

The range of possible articulations both in time and space that the editor commands gives his work huge potential. At its most dramatic the cut can pull the audience through the ages of the universe. The common practice of editing, however, is less explosive than in these special moments. Certain broad classes of style have emerged through the history of the cinema. As editing is an integral part of any film, a significant attempt to do something fresh with cinema is likely to require new achievements by the editor. It follows that there are many more styles of editing – for documentary, for films which use long takes and wide angle lenses, for others that use long takes and mobile cameras, for realist fictions, and so forth – than can be covered here. The three practices that are described below, however, are each chosen to suggest both the potential of cutting style and its limitations. Each in its time has been influential in establishing editing conventions.

Classic continuity cutting

This concept is not new to us because we have already mentioned some of the practices required to achieve this kind of 'invisible' style, the basic method of editing feature films developed in Hollywood. Cutting in this style is made to serve rather than dominate the narrative, and for this reason it becomes seemingly invisible. The story and the behaviour of the characters have right of way over everything else. Except for brief moments of exuberance when, say, a dramatic shot or a startling association of unexpected things grabs the attention, the style of the film is controlled so as not to obtrude upon the viewer's attention. In the editing process there are several keys to obtaining this near invisibility that leaves the illusion almost undisturbed. They include matching and motivating cuts, respecting the 'reading' rhythm, and adding to continuity through sound.

The matched cut
A cut is said to be matched when the visual characteristics of the start of the second shot follow in a way which the audience has learned to regard as 'natural' from the end of the first shot. Obviously a matched cut will have to observe the requirements of continuity sequencing: lighting, colour, characters must all match. But it requires more than this.

(1) If a character moves in a certain screen direction at the end of a shot, then at the start of the next shot he must be seen to be continuing in an appropriate direction. To take the simplest example, if he moves left to right and exits screen right, the audience will expect him to enter the next shot from screen left.

(2) Alternatively, an action begun in one shot but not completed is concluded in the next. A character is eating. In the first shot, a mid-shot, we see him lift a morsel from his plate, and as his hand rises we cut to a close-up and see him pop the food in his mouth. The beginning of the action in the first presupposes its completion in the second shot. The image is so composed that the movement both preserves a constant screen direction (bottom to top in this case), and centres on or tends towards the same area of the screen (in this case the middle).

(3) It will be recalled that the image is usually so composed that the viewer looks at one area rather than at the entire frame. If at the end of one shot the viewer's eyes are directed at, say, the top right of the frame, and at the start of the next he has to look bottom left, his eyes have to sweep across the screen, and that refocussing tends to be obtrusive. Shots which are well matched often keep the centre of attention either in

the same area or close to it. This requirement obviously clashes with the practice observed when movement continues through the frame wall (see (1) above). In that case the audience has long since learned to expect the re-entry of the character into the frame from the other side, and its expectations make the eye movement natural.

(4) Well-matched shots usually require a sufficient but not excessive change of image size. A cut between long and medium, or medium and close shots in either direction will work well because with the well-matched cut the reason for making the shot change is to reveal something in the second shot that could not be discerned in the first. A cut from long shot to close-up will often change the size of the object centred upon so much as to confuse the audience. Conversely a cut from say long shot to medium long shot provides very little new information and therefore the fact of making the cut becomes more evident to the eye than anything it might reveal. This last quality is characteristic of the 'jump cut' (see page 120).

(5) The angle of the shot should also in most cases be changed. Conventional wisdom holds that the camera should be moved through an angle of at least thirty degrees if two shots are to match. The argument is simple. It actually makes it easier to pick out from the background the actor or subject on which the shot is focussed if the angle changes. If it does not and the camera cuts to a point along the same axis the background as well as the subject enlarges or shrinks as the shot changes. Where the angle shifts adequately, a different background comes into the new shot and the viewer finds the original subject the only constant element between the shots, and does not, therefore, lose concentration.

The motivated cut

A cut is said to be motivated when what has occurred (either in the narrative or in the current shot) arouses a desire in the spectator to see something that is not at present visible. If at this point the shot changes so that desire is fulfilled, the interest of the spectator in what the film now reveals is such that the cut passes unremarked. This method of proceeding is fundamental to the classic Hollywood feature. It relies upon that simple desire to know what happens next that E. M. Forster identified as a basic organising impulse behind the enjoying (and the telling) of a story.*

In an establishing shot of a street we see a man catching up with another fellow. Who are they? What are they doing? We cut into a tight two-shot and can make out that one is much younger than the other, and that they are gesturing irritably at each other. Why? It goes without saying that the soundtrack will reveal this information as they mutter

*E. M. Forster, *Aspects of the Novel*, Penguin Books, Harmondsworth, 1962.

and growl at each other; but let us follow one possible sequence of shots to examine the kind of picture logic an editor might establish if he were wanting to motivate his cuts. We cut into a medium close shot of the younger man, and it is apparent from his angry face that he believes the other has wronged him. He accuses the older man of stealing his wallet. The accusation arouses in us an interest to know if this can be so, and we cut to a reaction shot of the other man, who looks defensive and sheepish. He tries to look wronged and waves the young man away. How does he in his turn respond? Another motivated cut brings us back to the earlier angle on the young man, who steps forward furiously. To do what? We cut back to the two-shot which shows him grabbing the thief by the arm. A big close-up of his hands shows the force of his grip, and we cut back to the two-shot as he frisks the thief. Will he find anything? Another big close-up shows his hands pulling a wallet out of the older man's pocket.

This illustration elaborates a simpler scene that we described when discussing privileged point of view (page 58). The connection is appropriate, for it is not difficult to see that the motivated cutting illustrated above actually has the effect of placing the spectator in the position he wants to be at any moment in the drama. In other words, in a story told in this manner the narrative motivates both the desire to make a cut at certain moments, and the wish to be placed in another position or point of view from which to see developments as clearly as possible. Motivated cutting and privileged point of view are intimately connected.

Reading and reaction

This same imagined scene shows not only how motivated cutting can work, it also demonstrates how it can bend time. For the scene takes much less time to play than the confrontation would in actuality have required. To take one moment only, the search of the thief is much shortened by the cut from the wider shot to the big close-up of the wallet. Narrative motivation of editing, the desire to know what happens next, is so strong it causes us to accept measurable time abridgement and concealed time reversal (see pages 111–12) as if they did not adjust normal flowing time. Of course now that we know that our own sense of the passing of time is a supple, flexible experience, this is less surprising than it might once have seemed.

We have seen that any shot or event takes time to digest (pages 75–6). This is not hard to understand if we think of it as a process of reading. Just as it takes a certain time to read a sentence, so it requires a certain period of time for our minds to make a reading of – and to understand – visual imagery. The more complicated the sentence, the longer it will take to read; the more complicated the information communicated by visual information, the longer that too will take to read – and we should add that the viewer of a film also requires time to react emotionally to what he sees and hears. Every editor has to have a strong intuitive sense of how long is required for a shot to communicate its information. In classic continuity editing he exploits that sense to add further to his audience's pleasure. He will not hold a shot so long that it begins to be boring; and he will not cut away from a shot before it has yielded all it has to communicate, unless, that is, he wishes to tease or excite.

A good film editor can stretch and compress time according to his audience's requirements of it at that particular point in the narrative (or, if he is working in some style other than classic continuity, he may choose to cheat or reverse audience expectation, holding shots for an unbearably long interval, for example). He deals not only with the present, allowing for reading and reaction, but also with the future in manipulating expectation. If we want to get on to the next event, he can shorten the time it takes us to get there (in the search for the wallet what we want to know is whether it is there, not what it is like to make a search of a person). Conversely, where for instance some ghastly scene appears to us to be totally inescapable, he can stretch time unbearably. We may not notice the mechanisms he uses, but we experience that dreadful, trapped suspense which the cinema creates so marvellously.

Sound in classic continuity editing

Sound can be employed to enhance the illusion. At the moment at which the shot cuts to a new image, the soundtrack can relate to the pictures in one of a number of ways.

(1) Sound and picture have been running in synchronisation, and as the picture cuts the sound cuts. At its most extreme this can be a drastic transition that plunges the audience without warning from one perhaps quiet scene into another which is very loud. It is then known as a 'hard cut'. The transition is more commonly less violent, and such simultaneous cutting of sound and vision is found often at the end of one scene and start of the next.

(2) As the picture cuts, the sound appears to continue uninterrupted. This mechanism makes the action seem uninterrupted, as the flowing, continuous sound reassures us that no time has been abridged despite the fact that it may indeed have been shortened. With a cut of this kind the wild tracks, providing background sound, run without interruption and assure us that the time represented is complete. The action is in fact fragmented into a number of shots, and time has been abridged in some and reversed in a concealed way in the transition between others. The synchronous soundtracks (dialogue and effects caused by visible action) weld the fragmented picture time to the apparently unbroken, continuous time of the wild track, and make the representation of time seem complete. Thus in our street scuffle, which abridged time

considerably, the wild track of general street sounds seems to assure us that time is represented in its entirety. The characters' words, footsteps, and scuffling noises link the fragmentary time of the shots to that seeming wholeness.

The running of uninterrupted sound across a picture cut is then a primary means of achieving flowing continuity. A simple variant occurs where an editor lets the sound run uninterrupted, but changes its level in accordance with the changed perspectives of the image. We look through a doorway at a seething crowd in a cocktail party, then cut to an angle within the room. As we do so the level of the noise is increased. By this means sound both serves to assure the audience of continuity, and confirms its changed point of view.

(3) The soundtrack is asynchronous to the image at the point of cutting. There is a large number of ways this device can be used, either in support of continuity editing, or to build alternative styles of film: the choice is too wide to make simple classification possible.

The well-rehearsed illusion

Classic continuity editing, then, does not actually render a perfect illusion. It deploys a number of devices and conventions with which we are now more than familiar as viewers, and they work towards increasing our pleasure. We add to that pleasure by accepting what they show us as a whole and seamless experience, and then we confirm our pleasure at deceiving ourselves by announcing that it is 'realistic'. But to emphasise just how far from the daily experience of life the classic continuity style can depart, we need look no further than at one of its most frequently used devices.

It will be recalled that 'parallel development' can occur when one scene is intercut with another (page 107). Two distinct but related events seem to be happening at the same time. The universal example of parallel development is the chase; this is so because that was how it was first put into service, to be repeated many thousands of times thereafter. Let us assume that in our earlier scene with the suspected thief, he breaks away from the young man as he leads him towards a police station. He runs off and tries to make his escape. As he runs the camera follows him, then cuts back to show the younger man racing in pursuit. As the chase continues the camera cuts between the two characters, until either they are brought together in one shot when the younger man catches the older, or one gets away from the other.

No device could be more disruptive of the audience's usual sense of its surroundings – now to be here, now hurled to another point, and then back again. Actually, parallel development has its origins in fiction rather than in fact: the nineteenth century novel also switched its readers between one scene and another – though less frequently than film does – and would leave one scene before it was complete, and then return to it before it had done with the second in its entirety. Paradoxically we often take this device, which so massively intrudes upon the smooth flow of time (for what we see as following the previous shot we are to take as coinciding with it), as a further example of the cinema's realism. Actually it is a further example of the cinema's power to complete a tightly packed narrative sequence, and therefore a further tribute to the power of film to create illusion.

While classic continuity editing attempts to give the sense of the completeness of the illusion it mediates to us, other styles of cutting deliberately set out to do the contrary and to keep their audiences aware that they are experiencing something cinematic rather than real. Of these the boldest example is the method of montage developed by Eisenstein.

Eisensteinian montage

If a method of editing is not given over to organising narrative as its main function, it may well be organised to give priority instead to ideas. This was Sergei Eisenstein's ambition in the cutting of his earlier films. Editing, he argued, should be infinitely more vigorous than in the classic continuity method. That method he likened to the brick by brick assembly of a wall, and found it just about as dull. Rather, editing should be characterised by collision, 'by the conflict of two pieces in opposition to each other' which should spark off new ideas.* Notice at once how different this style of editing must be from the continuity style with its ambitions towards achieving smoothness and imperceptibility.

The grounds for the conflict could be extremely broad. Successive shots might have opposing subjects, but conflict could equally well be expressed through the graphics of an image as through its themes. So a dark shot might be followed by a light one; movement towards the left could be followed by contrary movement to the right; one shape of composition could follow and utterly disrupt the shape established by the preceding shot; or the conflict could even lie in the rhythm of the shots.

In wishing to bring shots into collision, Eisenstein had something more in mind than creating mere chaos. It is worth recalling that he produced his early work in the immediate aftermath of the Soviet Revolution, an epoch which he and his colleagues found immensely productive and exciting. One of the central concepts on which Marxist thought relies – and which is worth bearing in mind when considering Eisenstein's technique – holds that conflict is a revitalising force,

*Sergei Eisenstein, 'The Cinematographic Principle and the Ideogram' in G. Mast and M. Cohen, *Film Theory and Criticism*, Oxford University Press, 2nd edn, 1979, pp. 85–100.

whether in society or in culture. From the conflict that arises between two sets of circumstances, or in the case of a communicating medium, between two statements (shots), there comes a new third thing, which is not either of the first two, but takes its origins from their collision. For Eisenstein, the collision between two shots was to yield not a third shot but an idea. That idea would be sparked by the collision of the two shots rather than belonging to either of them. He gave as an example of this kind of conflict at work the Japanese representational convention which puts together, for instance, the sign for an eye with the sign for water in order to give rise to the idea of weeping.

In Eisenstein's work this kind of construction is seen in many celebrated sequences. Kerensky, for example, in *October* (1928) pauses on the threshold of his office, and his supposed character as the new premier of Russia is indicated by repeated intercutting between his hesitation and the twirling and preening of a mechanical peacock. There is no motivation for this cut other than at the level of metaphor: the man is understood to be vain and ineffectual. Elsewhere in the same film a shot of an armoured tank being unloaded from its transporter as General Kornilov advances against the Bolsheviks is intercut with another shot of Red Guards crouching in a trench. The Guards are waiting miles away to resist Kornilov's advance. But as the tank is lowered towards the ground, repeated cutting between the two shots creates in the mind of the viewer the irresistible connection (the only available connection) that the tank, whose tracks seem visibly to descend towards the heads of the revolutionary soldiers, will grind down the Bolsheviks.

In both cases the relationship between two shots puts the viewer in a position where he must connect them in order to find a meaning that has no existence in either of the shots alone. If the viewer does not make a connection he can see no reason why the two shots should be intercut, and is puzzled. But equally typically of Eisenstein's montage, the viewer has very little freedom as to what meaning he draws from the connection: the two shots link together to spark off only one primary meaning. Thus while on the one hand the montage requires the viewer to respond to the stimuli provided by fragments of the film, on the other it controls his interpretation of their combination. Although this might seem to many familiar with Western culture to be a limitation, it attracted Eisenstein. As enthusiastic partisans of the revolutionary government, he and his colleagues meant to use cinema as an open instrument of propaganda, and to spread by its agency the messages and programmes of the new government to a population that was largely illiterate, and that had to be reached across a vast land mass. Although the intentions of other film makers may be quite different, Eisenstein's films are owed a large debt by much in cinema that runs counter to commercial mainstream movie-making. His stamp is to be found on many fine films of the last twenty years.

The French New Wave

Probably the most influential attempt in recent years to construct a style of editing counter to that of mainstream cinema was mounted by the directors of what is now called the French New Wave of the late 1950s and 1960s. Though it was not their original target, their work came to stand for a time as an indication of an alternative way of constructing films from the Hollywood style. But ultimately, for good reasons of their own, Hollywood producers simply absorbed aspects of the French style as a means of freshening up the appearance of their own films. In the process of incorporation into mainstream cinema, the French style was deprived of much of its original impact.

We have already referred to the location shooting and direct sound methods of some of the New Wave directors. Both Jean-Luc Godard and François Truffaut experimented at an early date with these methods. As they did so they began to develop new methods of cutting film together and new forms of plot logic as a means of ordering the construction of their films. They also set up new rhythmic patterns within their films and broke the familiar tempi of feature films.

One of the devices they used to upset old patterns was the 'jump cut'. The point about this kind of cut is that it is so mismatched as to be immediately noticeable, and it is thrust in at a point where classic continuity would lead us to expect either no cut at all or an invisible cut. A character might be in the middle of a speech to camera. This in itself was an innovation as the conventions of classic continuity require the actors to pretend that the audience does not exist, and, as a consequence, they never look at the camera. This shot would suddenly cut to another of the same character, in almost the same attitude, still talking to camera. The camera itself will have moved only just enough to make the change really disruptive. Characteristically the jump cut is made with a small, measurable movement either of subject or camera, and with an indefinite abridgement of time. This comes at a point in a scene where past practice would not have caused the viewer to expect any such cut into continuous time. In the hands of the New Wave directors it became a means for cutting out unnecessary time, and for *declaring* that the cut had been made. In subsequent years, however, the jump cut has become less obtrusive because television news and current affairs editors regularly cut film and tape this way.

The dissolve, as we have seen (page 103), took on new functions. And although the fade out and fade in did continue to indicate the end and start of scenes, they were not always used together. Now the editor might cut (to black, white, or even a colour), and fade in on the next scene. Alternatively he might fade out and cut in on the next shot.

By comparison with the familiar rhythms based on the viewer's speed of 'reading' that the style of classic continuity relied on, the rhythm of New Wave films at first seemed quirky. Where one of the long established principles of the Hollywood style was that the shot should be long enough on screen to make its point, but not a moment longer for fear of causing boredom, the New Wave directors relished standing that principle on its head. They would keep the camera running long after the narrative point had been made. Once the audience had got over the shock, it found that something more about one of the characters still in frame was being revealed. Occasionally nobody was in frame when the shot continued and the audience was left to contemplate how the mood of the place had affected the action, or *vice versa*.

The result of such rhythmic changes could be strange. At unexpected moments the audience found itself without any of the familiar things it expected to have to do. There might be no story to digest, and it might instead have to think about why a certain character had acted the way he did. What is more, the film might have come to a temporary halt, perhaps to give time for the problem to sink in. Then again, at other times, the cutting would speed through events in the characters' lives which the audience had grown to expect would be cherished. Romantic scenes, for instance, might not only be set in dingy locations with poor lighting, they also might be passed over in a quick and careless fashion. The audience had to get used to the idea that some screen directors did not see love in the glowing light with which Hollywood had usually flooded it. Here was a cinema attempting to reflect human experience in a way very different from the old, dominant model.

The authority of narrative

The fate of these revitalised methods of cutting film is instructive and reminds us that filmic conventions have a limited life and are not hard and fast rules. It also draws to our attention the dominant position of unambiguously narrative film in the cinema. The film makers working in Hollywood took over many of the devices developed by the European New Wave; but instead of having them disrupt narrative so they could do other things with their films, they absorbed them directly so that the long established story-telling logic of American cinema was hardly disturbed. The new devices became primarily ways of making surface changes to the films to keep their appearance fresh.

Dissolves, fades, cuts and the freeze frame all occur frequently in American cinema of the 1970s following the fashion in which they were employed in Europe. Many features of lighting and sound were also taken over wholesale. The jump cut, however, is not much used, probably because it so aggressively intrudes upon the sense of continuous time of each scene, and American narrative still prefers to respect that. Within the scene the old question-and-answer routine based on the desire to know what happens next still dominates. Between scenes, however, the arrival of European conventions has made some slight difference.

Before the European influence reached America, each successive scene in a film tended to be motivated by what had gone immediately before. In other words, something in the present scene would give rise to the need to move to the next, where either the narrative would be further complicated, or resolution of its complications would begin to be achieved. That regularly motivated progress from one scene to the next no longer always happens, and the spectator can find himself plunged into a new scene without knowing what is going on or why, because he has no information that relates to this new set of events. When this happens, the question the viewer wants answered is not 'What happens next?', but 'What brought this about?' In other words, the way the scenes have been connected encourages him, not to look forward to the next event, but to look backward to what happened last. There he seeks a cause of present events.

It has to be said at once that mainline American cinema does not usually withhold the answer to this new question for very long. As ever, producers fear that the audience may not wish to have to think for themselves; it seems a safer bet to tell them. So the narrative commonly steps in quickly to make sure that everything is explained. Thus, having adopted a device that encourages the audience to look at causes of cinematic events a little more deeply, American producers simultaneously defused it. The viewer quickly learns that he does not need to puzzle things out for himself; patience will bring him the information he needs, or at least enough to reassure him that no further effort on his part is called for.

When we recall that films of the kind we have been describing are made for release in cinemas, and that they are usually more adventurous in their structure than the dominant form of American screen fiction, the television series, it becomes apparent to what extent the self-contained narrative dominates our experience of the screen. This is not to claim that films in which the spectator is urged to sit back and consume dominate the cinemas and television screens of every nation. However, it is true of most feature films and television drama series produced in the English language by the big institutions. There are good reasons for the existence of this state of affairs, and the causes are to be sought in economic, cultural and social forces. The investigation of those forces, however, must be the subject of other books.

Part 6

Suggestions for further reading

ARIJON, DANIEL: *Grammar of the Film Language*, Focal Press, London, 1976. A detailed account of the potential of continuity cutting.

BORDWELL, DAVID and THOMPSON, KRISTIN: *Film Art*, Addison-Wesley, London, 1979. An introduction to the study of film, with a chapter on film history.

BURCH, NOËL: *Theory of Film Practice*, Secker & Warburg, London, 1973. A film maker's analysis of the way narrative films are structured, and suggestions for ways in which current practices might be radically altered.

MAST, GERALD and COHEN, MARSHALL (EDS.): *Film Theory and Criticism*, Oxford University Press, Oxford, 2nd edn, 1979. A comprehensive anthology of articles and extracts providing a useful introduction to the theory and criticism of films.

MONACO, JAMES: *How to Read a Film*, Oxford University Press, New York, 1979. An ambitious but sometimes sketchy survey of the history of film; the processes of mediation through film; film theory; and film as a signifying system.

PERKINS, VICTOR F.: *Film as Film*, Penguin, Harmondsworth, 1972. Well argued case for considering film as a medium with its own quite distinct qualities.

PLACE, J. A. and PETERSON, L. S.: 'Some Visual Motifs of Film Noir', *Film Comment*, Vol 10.i, January 1974, pp.30–5. Exemplary application of film aesthetics to an established genre.

REISZ, KAREL and MILLAR, GAVIN: *The Technique of Film Editing*, Focal Press, London, 2nd edn, 1968. The best account of the way the work of the film editor guides the perception of the film viewer.

REYNERTSON, A. J.: *The Work of the Film Director*, Focal Press, London, 1970. Good but slightly out-of-date account of the director's opportunities for the control of his medium.

STEPHENSON, RALPH and DEBRIX, J. R.: *The Cinema as Art*, Penguin, Harmondsworth, 1970. Provides the reader with a relatively simple account of the way in which the film maker controls and shapes the viewer's perceptions of space and time.

Index

York Handbooks: list of titles

YORK HANDBOOKS form a companion series to York Notes and are designed to meet the wider needs of students of English and related fields. Each volume is a compact study of a given subject area, written by an authority with experience in communicating the essential ideas to students of all levels.

The author of this Handbook

JOHN IZOD was born in England and educated at Prince Edward School, Harare City. He graduated in English at the University of Leeds and subsequently obtained the degree of Ph. D. there. From 1969 to 1978 he lectured in English at the New University of Ulster, where he helped to introduce a degree in Communication Studies. Since 1978 he has been in charge of Film and Media Studies at the University of Stirling — as Head of Department and Senior Lecturer from 1985. He has published various articles and is the author of *Hollywood and the Box Office, 1895 — 1986,* a book on the business side of the American film industry.